Revising
Prose

RICHARD A. LANHAM

UNIVERSITY OF CALIFORNIA, LOS ANGELES

Revising Prose

Second Edition

MACMILLAN PUBLISHING COMPANY
NEW YORK
COLLIER MACMILLAN PUBLISHERS
LONDON

Macmillan Publishing Company
866 Third Avenue, New York, New York 10022

Collier Macmillan Canada, Inc.

Library of Congress Cataloging-in-Publication Data

Lanham, Richard A.
  Revising prose.

  1. English language—Style.   2. English language—
Rhetoric.   3. Editing.   I. Title.
PE1421.L297   1987   808'.042   86-12696
ISBN 0-02-367440-7

Printing: 2 3 4 5 6 7   Year: 7 8 9 0 1 2 3

ISBN 0-02-367440-7

Preface

The more student papers I read, the more I think that America's current epidemic verbal ineptitude comes on two levels, rudimentary and stylistic. The rudimentary level is caused by a failure to teach simple functional literacy. Students on this level make mistakes from ignorance. They don't know the rules. On the stylistic level, though, something different happens. You are not so much making "writing errors" as trying, usually with indifferent success, to imitate a predominant style, one you see all around you. This style, which let's call "the Official Style," you'll find, too, in your textbooks and in the academic bureaucracy's official pronouncements. Naturally enough, you come to think that's what is expected of you and try to imitate it.

Revising Prose addresses this second, stylistic level of the verbal epidemic. It is concerned not with inspiration or argumentation but with stylistic revision. Maybe *translation* would be a better word—translating the Official Style into plain English. *Revising Prose* tries to make you self-conscious about what the Official Style is, what it means to write it, and how it can—and usually should—be translated into plain English. The Official Style comes in several dialects—bureaucratic, social-scientific, lab report scientific, computer-engineering-military—but all exhibit the same basic attributes. They all build on the same central imbalance, a dominance of nouns and an atrophy of verbs, the triumph of stasis over action. This basic imbalance is easy to cure—if you want to cure it.

But when *do* you want to cure it? Students today often feel—sometimes with justification—that they will be penalized for writing plain English. In the academic bureaucracy, writing plain English seems like walking down the hall with nothing on. Such public places demand protective coloration. Furthermore, if you are going to write in the Official Style, how do you make sure you are writing a good and not a bad one? And if the Official Style is, all said and done, a bad prose style—and it is—what, then, can "good" and "bad" mean when applied to prose?

Revising Prose starts out by teaching revision. When you've learned how to do that, we'll reflect on what such revision is likely to do for you—and to you—in the bureaucratic world of the future. We ought then to be able to see what "good" and "bad" mean for prose, and what you are really doing when you revise.

People often argue that writing cannot be taught, and if they mean that inspiration cannot be commanded nor laziness banished, then of course they are right. But stylistic analysis—revision—is something else, a method, not a mystical rite. How we compose—pray for the muse, marshall our thoughts, find the willpower to glue backside to chair—these may be idiosyncratic, but revision belongs to the public domain. Anyone can learn it.

I've called my basic procedure for revision the Paramedic Method because it provides emergency therapy, a first-aid kit, not the art of medicine. The only real solution to America's literacy crisis is a mature and reflective training in verbal self-awareness. Once you have this, you'll see and correct ordinary mistakes almost in passing. If you don't have it, no amount of rule memorization will bring good prose. For prose style, like the rest of human experience, is too various to be adequately described by rules. We don't write by rule but by imitation—as you've no doubt found when you've tried your hand at the Official Style.

But you can't stop the world to get off and take a course in prose style. The paper is due next week. And so *Revising*

Prose. It is intended to be a self-teaching text to accompany courses that require papers. Like paramedicine in underdeveloped countries, it does not attempt to teach a full body of knowledge but only to diagnose and cure existing disease. No one argues that the paramedic is equal to the doctor but only that he may be equal to the disease.

Since my classroom students no longer seem to know the basic terms of grammar, I've listed them in an Appendix. The prose examples used—the "Jim kicks Bill" paradigm excepted—all come from student papers or from writing in what, with some exaggeration, is called "the real world."

An electronic revolution has occurred since the first edition of *Revising Prose*. I've tried to acknowledge it in the second edition, as much as a practical, hands-on manual like this can do so, by adding a chapter that at least suggests the enormous changes the personal computer brings to prose composition and revision. To keep the book short—shortness being, by all accounts, one of its primary virtues—I've cut two chapters, "Voice and Sound Feedback," and "The School Style," and tried to accommodate their essence elsewhere. I have also changed many examples, both for variety and to reflect a wider range of student and teacher writing than the first edition's "English Department" bias permitted.

Revising Prose has met the pleasing fate of being used in unexpected and unintended ways. I originally designed it to be a "self-teaching text to accompany courses that require papers." It was intended for American undergraduate students but speedily came to be used by graduate students as well and, at the opposite end of the scale, to serve as a freshman text too. Business schools seemed to find it useful and, beyond the university, training programs in business and government as well. I have tried, over the last several years, to respond to these flattering uses in ways that would not lengthen the book or complicate its argument. In the second edition, for example, I've included more graduate student and professorial writing so that the undergraduate focus has widened somewhat. The book should now better suit graduate classes, especially classes that train teaching assistants to teach writing. For business applications, I produced *Revising Business Prose,* itself now scheduled to appear in a second edition. For government writing, I have written *Revising Government Prose.* And, if the gods give leisure, versions for technical and legal writing may see daylight.

A book like *Revising Prose* cannot by itself serve for a Freshman Composition course. I have tried though, in the last several years, to supply ancillary components that might broaden its usefulness there. Michael Cohen and I have published a computer program, HOMER, which takes advantage of the highly computerizable nature of the Paramedic Method. I have also written two half-hour video cassettes, *Revising Prose* and *Revising Business Prose,* which use digital videographics to illustrate the book's revision techniques. In addition, I have prepared workbooks for both *Revising Prose* and *Revising Business Prose.* Finally, I have recently published an introductory guide to the theory and practice of prose analysis, *Analyzing Prose;* I hope it will be used for advanced composition courses and graduate courses in prose analysis, and as an advanced "teacher's guide" for the *Revising Prose* books. In *Analyzing Prose,* I sketch out the full theory of which the Paramedic Method forms a small part.

I hope that all of these "texts," printed and electronic, may serve as an informal delivery system for teaching *Revising Prose* in the many different classrooms where it seems to have found a home.

A word on the Paramedic Method (PM). It works only if you *follow* it rather than *argue* with it. When it tells you to get rid of the prepositional phrases, get rid of them. Don't go into a "but, well, in this case, given my style, really I need to . . ." bob and weave. You'll never learn anything that way. The PM constitutes the center of this book. Use it. Clip out p. xiv and tack it above your desk for easy reference.

R. A. L.

Acknowledgments

My UCLA colleagues Carol Hartzog, Joyce Peterson, and Edward Condren kindly read the draft of the first edition and tried it out in class. I must now, for suggestions about the second edition, thank many of my colleagues in the UCLA Writing Programs. And I must again thank the UCLA students who provided the examples—and the incentive first to write and then to revise *Revising Prose*.

Contents

The Paramedic Method

1. Circle the prepositions.
2. Circle the "is" forms.
3. Ask "Who is kicking who?"
4. Put this "kicking" action in a simple (not compound) active verb.
5. Start fast—no mindless introductions.
6. Write out each sentence on a blank sheet of paper and mark off its basic rhythmic units with a "/".
7. Read the passage aloud with emphasis and feeling.
8. Mark off sentence lengths in the passage with a "/".

CHAPTER 1

Who's Kicking Who?

No student these days feels comfortable writing simply "Jim kicks Bill." The system seems to require something like "One can easily see that a kicking situation is taking place between Bill and Jim." Or, "This is the kind of situation in which Jim is a kicker and Bill is a kickee." Jim cannot enjoy kicking Bill; no; for school use, it must be "Kicking Bill is an activity hugely enjoyed by Jim." Absurdly contrived examples? Here are some real ones:

This sentence is in need of an active verb.

Physical satisfaction is the most obvious of the consequences of premarital sex.

In strict contrast to Watson's ability to control his mental stability through this type of internal gesture, is Rosalind Franklin's inability to even conceive of such "playing."

See what they have in common? They are like our Bill and Jim examples, assembled from strings of prepositional phrases glued together by that all-purpose epoxy "is." In each case the sentence's verbal force has been shunted into a noun and for a verb we make do with "is," the neutral copulative, the weakest verb in the language. Such sentences project no

1

life, no vigor. They just "are." And the "is" generates those strings of prepositional phrases fore and aft. It's so easy to fix. Look for the real action. Ask yourself, who's kicking who? (Yes, I know, it should be *whom,* but doesn't it sound stilted?)

In "This sentence is in need of an active verb," the action obviously lies in "need." And so, "This sentence needs an active verb." The needless prepositional phrase "in need of," simply disappears once we see who's kicking who. The sentence, animated by a real verb, comes alive, and in six words instead of nine.

Where's the action in "Physical satisfaction is the most obvious of the consequences of premarital sex"? Buried down there in "satisfaction." But just asking the question reveals other problems. Satisfaction isn't really a *consequence* of premarital sex, in the same way that, say, pregnancy is. And, as generations of women will attest, sex, premarital or otherwise, does not always satisfy. Beyond all this, the contrast between the clinical phrasing of the sentence, with its lifeless "is" verb, and the lifegiving power of "lust in action" makes the sentence seem almost funny. Excavating the action from "satisfaction" yields "Premarital sex satisfies! Obviously!" This gives us a lard factor of 66% and a comedy factor even higher. (You find the lard factor by dividing the difference between the number of words in the original and the revision by the number of words in the original. In this case, $12 - 4 = 8$; $8 \div 12 = .66$. If you've not paid attention to your own writing before, think of a lard factor (LF) of one-third to one-half as normal and don't stop revising until you've removed it. The comedy factor in prose revision, though often equally great, does not lend itself to numerical calculation.) But how else do we revise here? "Premarital sex is fun, obviously" seems a little better, but we remain in thrall to "is." And the frequent falsity of the observation stands out yet more. Revision has exposed the empty thinking. The student makes it even worse by continuing: "Some degree of physical satis-

2

faction is present in almost all coitus." Add it all together and we get something like, "People usually enjoy premarital sex" (LF, 79%). At its worst, academic prose makes us laugh by describing ordinary reality in extraordinary language.

The student writing about James Watson's *The Double Helix* stumbles on the standard form of absent-minded academic prose: a string of prepositional phrases and infinitives, then a lame "to be" verb, then more prepositional phrases and infinitives. Look at the structure:

> *In* strict contrast
>> *to* Watson's ability
>> *to* control his mental stability
>> *through* this type
>> *of* internal gesture,
>> *is* Rosalind Franklin's inability
>> *to* even conceive
>> *of* such "playing."

Notice how long this laundry list takes to get going? The root action skulks down there in "ability to control." So we revise: "Watson controls himself through these internal gestures; Rosalind Franklin does not even know such gestures exist." I've removed "in strict contrast" because the rephrasing clearly implies it. I've given the sentence two simple root verbs—"controls" and "knows." And I've used the same word—"gestures"—for the same concept in both phrases to make the contrast tighter and easier to see. We've reduced seven prepositional phrases and infinitives to one prepositional phrase, and thus banished that DA-da-da, DA-da-da monotony of the original. A lard factor of 41% but, more important, we've given the sentence shape; some life flows from its verbs.

The drill for this problem stands clear. Circle every form of "to be" ("is," "was," "will be," "seems to be") and every

3

prepositional phrase. Then find out who's kicking who and start rebuilding the sentence with that action. Two prepositional phrases in a row turn on the warning light, three make a problem, and four invite disaster. With a little practice, sentences like "The mood Dickens paints is a bleak one" will turn into "Dickens paints a bleak mood" (LF 38%) almost before you've written them.

Prepositional phrase strings do not, of course, always come from undergraduates. Look at these "of" strings from a linguist, a literary critic, and a popular gourmet:

> It is the totality *of* the interrelation *of* the various components *of* language and the other communication systems which is the basis for referential memory.

> These examples *of* unusual appropriateness *of* the sense *of* adequacy to the situation suggest the primary signification *of* rhyme in the usual run *of* lyric poetry.

> Frozen breads and frozen pastry completed the process *of* depriving the American woman *of* the pleasure *of* boasting *of* her baking.

The "of" strings are the worst of all. They look like a child pulling a gob of bubble gum out into a long string. When you try to revise them, you can feel how fatally easy the "is and of" formulation can be for expository prose. And how fatally confusing, too, since to find an active, transitive verb for "is" means, often, adding a specificity the writer has not provided. So, in the first example, what does "is the basis for" really mean? And does the writer mean that language's components interact with "other communication systems," or is he talking about "components" of "other communication systems" as well? The "of" phrases refer back to those going before in so general a way that you can't keep straight what really modifies what. So revision here is partly a guess.

Referential meaning emerges when the components of language interact with other communication systems.

Or the sentence might mean

Referential meaning emerges when the components of language interact with the components of other communication systems.

Do you see the writer's problem? He has tried to be more specific than he needs to be, to build his sentence on a noun ("totality") that demands a string of "of's" to qualify it. Ask where the action is, build the sentence on a *verb,* and the "totality" follows as an implication. Noun-centeredness like this generates most of our present-day prose sludge.

The second example, out of context, doesn't make much sense. Perhaps "These examples, where adequacy to the situation seems unusually appropriate, suggest how rhyme usually works in lyric poetry." The third is easy to fix. Try it.

In asking who's kicking who, a couple of mechanical tricks come in handy. Besides getting rid of the "is's" and changing every passive voice ("is defended by") to an active voice ("defends"), you can squeeze the compound verbs hard, make every "are able to" into a "can," every "seems to succeed in creating" into "creates," every "cognize the fact that" (no, I didn't make it up) into "think," every "am hopeful that" into "hope," every "provides us with an example of" into "exemplifies," every "seeks to reveal" into "shows," and every "there is the inclusion of" into "includes."

And you can amputate those mindless introductory phrases, "The fact of the matter is that" and "The nature of the case is that." Start fast and then, as they say in the movies, "cut to the chase" as soon as you can. Instead of "the answer is in the negative," you'll find yourself saying "No."

5

We now have the beginnings of the Paramedic Method (PM):

1. Circle the prepositions.
2. Circle the "is" forms.
3. Ask "Who is kicking who?"
4. Put this "kicking" action in a simple (not compound) active verb.
5. Start fast—no mindless introductions.

Let's use the PM on a more complex instance of blurred action, the opening sentences of a psych paper:

The history of Western psychological thought has long been dominated by philosophical considerations as to the nature of man. These notions have dictated corresponding considerations of the nature of the child within society, the practices by which children were to be raised, and the purposes of studying the child.

Two actions there—"dominate" and "dictate"—but neither has fully escaped from its native stone. The prepositional phrase and infinitive strings just drag them down.

The history
  of Western psychological thought
  by philosophical considerations
  as to the nature
  of man
  . . .
  of the nature
  of the child
  within society
  by which children
  to be raised
  of studying

We next notice, in asking "Who is kicking who?," all the *incipient* actions lurking in the nouns: *thinking* in "thought," *consider* in "considerations," more *thinking* somewhere in "notions." They hint at actions they don't supply and thus blur the actor–action relationship still further. We want, remember, a plain active verb, no prepositional phrase strings, and the natural actor firmly in charge. The actor must be "philosophical considerations as to the nature of man;" the verb "dominates;" the object of the action "the history of Western psychological thought." Now the real problems emerge. What does "philosophical considerations as to the nature of man" really mean? Buried down there is *a question:* "What is the nature of man?" The "philosophical considerations" just blur this question rather than narrow it. Likewise, the object of the action—"the history of Western psychological thought"—can be simply "Western psychological thought." Shall we put all this together in the passive form that the writer used? "Western psychological thought has been dominated by a single question: what is the nature of man?" Or, with an active verb, "A single question has dominated Western psychological thought: what is the nature of man?" Our formulaic concern with the stylistic surface—passives, prepositional phrases, kicker and kickee—has led here to a much more focused *thought*.

The first sentence passes its baton very awkwardly to the second. "Considerations," confusing enough as we have seen, become "these notions" at the beginning of the second sentence, and these "notions," synonymous with "considerations" in the first sentence, dictate more but different "considerations" in the second. We founder in these vague and vaguely synonymous abstractions. Our unforgiving eye for prepositional phrases then registers "*of* the nature *of* the child *within* society." We don't need "within society;" where else will psychology study children? And "the nature of the child" telescopes to "the child." We metamorphose "the practices by which children were to be raised" into "child-rearing," and

7

"the purposes in studying the child" leads us back to "corresponding considerations of the nature of the child within society," which it seems partly to overlap. But we have now a definite actor, remember, in the first sentence—the "single question." So a tentative revision: "The same basic question has dictated three subsequent ones: What are children like? How are they to be raised? Why should we study them?" Other revisions suggest themselves. Work a couple out. In mine, I've used "question" as the baton passed between the two sentences because it clarifies the relationship between the two. And I've tried to expose what real, clear action lay hidden beneath the conceptual cotton-wool of "these notions have dictated corresponding considerations."

This two-sentence example of student academic prose rewards some reflection. First, the sentences *make no grammatical or syntactical mistakes*. Second, *they need not have come from a student*. Any issue of a psychology journal or text will net you a dozen from the same mold. Third, not one in a thousand TAs or professors reading this prose will think anything is wrong with it. Just the opposite. It reads just right; it sounds professional. The teacher's comment on this paper reads, in full: "An excellent paper—well conceived, well organized and well written—A + ." Yet it makes clear neither its main actor nor action; its thought consistently blurs in vague general concepts like "considerations," "notions," and the like; and the cradle-rocking monotony of its rhythm puts us to sleep. It reveals a mind writing in formulae, out of focus, putting no pressure on itself. The student is not thinking so much as, on a scale slightly larger than normal, *filling in the blanks*. You can't build bridges thinking in this muddled way; they will fall down. If you bemuse yourself thus in a chemistry lab, you'll blow up the apparatus. And yet the student, obviously very bright, has been invited to write this way and is rewarded for it. He or she has been doing a stylistic imitation, and has brought if off successfully. Chances are great that the focused, plain-language version I've offered will get a much lower grade than the original. Revision is always perilous and paradoxical, but nowhere more so than in the academic world. We'll revert to both perils and paradoxes as we proceed.

CHAPTER 2

Sentences and Shopping Bags

Official Style sentences seldom come in any shape. They just go on and on, as if they were emerging from a nonstop sausage machine. This shapelessness makes them unreadable: you cannot read them aloud with expressive emphasis. Try to. When language as spoken and heard has completely atrophied, the sentence becomes less a shaped unit of emphatic utterance than a shopping bag of words. Read your own prose aloud and with emphasis—or better still, have a friend read it to you. This rehearsal can often tell you more about the shape, rhythm, and emphasis of your sentences than any other single device. You might try, too, writing a single sentence on a sheet of blank paper. Forget your profound meaning for a minute and just look at the sentence's shape. Try to isolate the basic parts and trace their relationship to one another.

We'll begin with a little cocktail sausage: "For today's audience the demand is for motion pictures and television." Four equal units glued together:

> For today's audience
> the demand is
> for motion pictures
> and television.

Actor: "today's audience." Action: "wants." Object: "movies and TV." All three together; central verb "wants" in the middle.

REVISION:

Today's audience wants movies and TV. (LF 45%)

Another example, for contrast: "The author will throw a noun or two at you, wait for your reaction, then throw a few more at you." Perfect. A believable voice, a nice A-B-A shape. Nothing needed here except applause.

Often the shopping bag sentence will begin with a dead-rocket opening that stuffs everything in before the main verb and thus finds its action only when about to expire:

> The manner in which behavior first shown in a conflict situation may become fixed so that it persists after the conflict has passed is then discussed.

> The manner (monstrous filling) is discussed.

No actor is given by "is discussed," so we'll invent one. "Prof. Guffbag then discusses how behavior, which first emerges in conflict, persists after the conflict has passed." First the actor, then the action, then two balanced and parallel elements:

> Prof. Guffbag then discusses
> how behavior, which emerges in conflict,
> persists after the conflict has passed.

The balance and parallel in "emerges–conflict" and "persists–conflict" glue the two elements together. The sentence begins fast, then leads us to a garden whose simple design we can easily comprehend.

12

Here is a classic shopping bag from a famous historian:

There is one last point in the evidence of Everard of Ypres which deserves a comment before we leave it. This is the very surprising difference between the number of students at Gilbert's lectures in Chartres and in Paris. The small number in Chartres is perhaps not surprising, for Gilbert was a notoriously difficult lecturer; but the very large number in Paris is very surprising. Of course, it is possible to give several different explanations of these figures, but since the authority for both numbers is the same and there was no obvious reason for distortion, they should, at least provisionally, be treated seriously.

The absolute formula: strings of prepositional phrases glued together by "is":

There *is* one last point
   in the evidence
   of Everard
   of Ypres which deserves a comment before we leave it.
This *is*
   the very surprising difference
   between the number
   of students
   at Gilbert's lectures
   in Chartres and
   in Paris.

No need to continue this charting; you get the idea. The writer, like a bag-boy at the grocery store, stuffs his sentence with first one prepositional phrase and then another until the basket of his thoughts stands empty. Revision? I'll try revising the first two sentences into one: "One last question apropos Everard of Ypres: why did so few students attend his Chartres lectures and so many those in Paris?" (LF 44%; 2 prepositions instead of 7).

13

Now a monster—a Polish sausage of a sentence—by a well-known sociologist. Any student studying the social sciences will have to read acres of such prose:

> The fact that all selves are constituted by or in terms of the social process, and are individual reflections of it—or rather of this organized behavior pattern which it exhibits, and which they comprehend in their respective structures—is not in the least incompatible with or destructive of the fact that every individual self has its own peculiar individuality, its unique pattern; because each individual within that process, while it reflects in its organized structure the behavior patterns of that process as a whole, does so from its own particular and unique standpoint within that process, and thus reflects in its organized structure a different aspect or perspective of this whole social behavior pattern from that which is reflected in the organized structure of any other individual self within that process (just as every monad in the Leibnizian universe mirrors that universe from a different point of view, and thus mirrors a different aspect or perspective of that universe).

None of the usual definitions of a sentence really says much, but every sentence ought somehow to organize a pattern of thought, even if it does not always reduce that thought to bite-sized pieces. This shapeless hippo, however, has at heart only our getting lost. Notice how far it is from the first subject ("the fact that") to its verb ("is")? We forget the subject before we get to the verb. To bring some shape to this shopping bag, we'll need, for a start, a full stop after "pattern." "The fact that" translates, as always, into "that." And then we return to changing passive voice to active voice ("are constituted by" to "constitutes"), to eliminating prepositional phrases, to finding out where the action is (who is kicking who). And we must attack, too, the compulsive pattern of needless overspecification ("incompatible with, or destructive

14

of"), the endemic curse of academic writing from the cradle to the grave. So: "That society (= "the social process") constitutes all selves and they reflect it. . . ." So far so good. What of the two lines between—and—? They simply restate, in new gobbledgook terminology, what has preceded. Shred them. And "is not in the least incompatible with or destructive of the fact that" translates into English as "does not in the least destroy." "Every individual self has its own peculiar individuality, its own unique pattern" = "the unique self." We have translated the first half of this shopping bag back into English as:

> That society constitutes all selves and they reflect it, does not in the least destroy the unique self. (18 words instead of 65; LF 72%)

To finish shaping this sentence, we need only add a comma after "selves." Now read it aloud. Subject ("That society constitutes all selves") separated from its verb by only a short parenthetical addition ("and they reflect it") stays in our mind until we reach a direct object ("the unique self"), which falls into the naturally emphatic closing position. The voice ought to rise in pitch for the parenthetic "they reflect" and for "least" and "unique." The sentence shape underscores its meaning rather than burying it. The syntax permits, encourages, the voice to help. The prose has become readable. See if you can clean up the rest of the passage in the same way.

Looking for the natural shape of a sentence often suggests the quickest way to revision. Consider this example:

> I think that all I can usefully say on this point is that in the normal course of their professional activities social anthropologists are usually concerned with the third of these alternatives, while the other two levels are treated as raw data for analysis.

15

The action starts with "are usually concerned with." Beginning to build a shape means starting here. "Usually, social anthropologists concentrate on the third alternative. . . ." And now, do we really need the whole endless dead-rocket opening, from "I think" to "activities"? "In the normal course of their professional activities" = "usually," and the rest is guff. So: "Usually, social anthropologists concentrate on the third alternative and treat the other two as raw data" ("for analysis" being implied by "raw data"). A final polishing moves "usually" to the other side of "social anthropologists" so as to modify "concentrate" more immediately. The sentence then begins strongly, subject—short modifer—verb, and offers two other emphasis points, "third alternative" and "raw data." And shouldn't we subordinate the "treat" by turning it into a participle? The final revision would then read, "Social anthropologists usually concentrate on the third alternative, treating the other two as raw data." Read it aloud now and then go back to the original and compare (15 words instead of 45; LF 66%).

Confused. Confusing. Two-thirds longer than it should be. What would a mistake of this magnitude look like in another area of human endeavor? A builder who needs three yards of concrete and orders nine? A physician who mistakes the drug and triples the dose? American college students read a steady diet of this prose—often textbook prose is *all* they read. Two lessons, at least, are thus taught: first, often you can't understand the assignment, at least not *really,* so just skim it; second, *don't,* therefore, *really pay attention to the words.* Words on a page do not mean things explicitly. They only point to generalized meanings in vague formulas.

And so a student writes: "The most important thing to remember is the fact that interest in the arts has not declined in popularity," instead of "Interest in the arts has not declined." Or "The generation of television is a feeble one, it is a generation lacking in many areas, especially that of artistic background and interest." Here, of course, we don't know whether it is television that is being generated, or an age-group being generated by it. And who knows what "artistic background and interest" means, or what the "many areas" might be. So revision becomes both a guess and a satire: "The TV generation has shown little interest in art, or in anything else either." Such a sentence shows not bad writing so much as a listless imitation of the vague, approximative prose the student reads in textbooks. The imitation often becomes exactly formulaic, as in "Heartfelt House has earned a reputation for excellence for the sharing of the wisdom of the path of compassionate service in the natural healing arts." Easy to see the string of prepositional phrases, but you have to ponder the sentence to see the damage done to what might otherwise have been a thought. What is Heartfelt House good at? Excellence? Sharing? Wisdom? Path? Compassionate service? Healing arts? Does it all add up to "Heartfelt House has a good reputation as a nursing home"?

What about this sentence?

> Throughout our lives, we are exposed to a lot of different teachings and one of them, in our society, is the value placed upon a life in which we are successful.

Easy to revise:

> Our society teaches the value of success. (LF 77%)

The rest is just floor-shavings, left after the thought has been turned on the lathe. But the Official Style always includes the floor-shavings, feels undressed without them, and so this student prose does too. When you cherish the floor-shavings of thought, you spell out the obvious: "The UCLA Premed Handbook states that a principle premed question is whether or not to become a physician." Even to say that writing

17

contains needless clichés becomes "Both articles contain several words and phrases that, because of their ambiguous or cliché property, could easily be omitted."

This kind of prose does not come naturally. You have to learn it. And with it comes a habit of reading. Or, rather, this kind of prose asks to be read in a certain way—quick, inattentive, just for the general drift, the fugitive generalization you highlight in paragraph four—that invites you to write prose of the same kind. Shopping bag sentences display more than shapeless verbal jumbles, maddening verbosity, and the floor-shavings of aborted thoughts, off-putting as these are. A whole way of reading and thinking stands revealed; vague, unfocused, built on temporary generalities themselves built on hopelessly cluttered heaps of general terms, often ending in -ion "shun" words. When a philosophy student writes, "In the sixth *Meditation,* Descartes comes to the conclusion that the mind is distinct from the body," instead of "In the sixth *Meditation* Descartes distinguishes the mind from the body," she stands more than a passive away from the tenor and timbre of Descartes' thought. A whole style, the Official Style, away. And the Official Style has become today, more often than not, the Academic Style.

The Paramedic Method tries to focus attention on the distortions of the Official Style by using simple diagnostic questions. Let's review it, as developed to date.

1. Circle the prepositions.
2. Circle the "is" forms.
3. Ask "Who is kicking who?"
4. Put this "kicking action" in a simple (not compound) active verb.
5. Start fast—no mindless introductions.

Now we'll put the PM to work on an undergraduate paragraph that considers the subject itself—prose.

A piece of prose may be considered sincere if, in some manner, it establishes its credibility to its audience. The degree of sincerity, however, is relative to the type of person reading it. A logical, scientific person would feel gratified if the author included the relationship of counterpoints to his message. To them this technique shows that the author considered opposing viewpoints while presenting his own; an analytical ideal for such an audience.

A typical piece of shapeless prose. Tedious. Lifeless. Just plain boring to read. The first sentence ought by its shape to underline the basic contrast of "sincere" with "credible." How about, "Prose will seem sincere if it seems credible"? The parallelism of "seems sincere" and "seems credible" works because the two parallel elements stand close together. Sparks can fly between them. The sentence gains some snap, a shape (8 words instead of 19; LF 58%). Now for the second sentence. It qualifies the first and should do so obviously. We need an adversative, "but": "But how sincere will depend on the type of reader." Or maybe just "on the reader," "type of" and "kind of" being usually expendable qualifiers. Now read the last two sentences aloud, and with feeling—*con amore*. Can't be done. Where, though, does your voice *want* to rise, what does it *want* to stress? Obviously "a logical scientific person" and "opposing viewpoints." What shape will model this? "A logical, scientific person" = "A scientist"; "would feel gratified" = "would welcome"; "if the other included the relationship of counterpoints to his message" = "would welcome a statement of alternative views." In the last sentence, "to them" refers back, impossibly enough, to a singular antecedent ("scientific person") and the rest is inane repetition. What follows after the semicolon represents dieselizing—the prose engine continuing to run after the key has been turned off. It indicates that a sense of shape means a feeling for strong closings as well as strong openings. As a

19

revision, then: "A scientist would welcome a statement of alternative views" (9 words for 40; LF 78%). And for the whole passage:

> Prose will seem sincere if it seems credible. But how sincere will depend on the (type of) reader. A scientist would welcome a statement of alternative views.

We've solved a number of problems but we've created some too, first in the sequence of thought and, scarcely less obviously, in the rhythmic interrelation of the three sentences. The prose sounds choppy. It often happens in elephantiasis surgery like this and can't be helped. Don't worry. Concentrate on the shape of each sentence. If, as here, you end up with a string of sentences all the same length, this can be fixed later.

To articulate the sequence of thought, we need to join the first two sentences and acknowledge the third as an example:

> Prose will seem sincere if it seems cred . . .

Now the real problem emerges. What depends *directly* on the reader is credibility, not sincerity. The writer was trying to say: "Prose will seem sincere if it seems credible, but how credible will depend on who reads it." "Who reads it" finally gets around the awkward "type of" problem and leads directly to "A scientist." Now that we've gotten this straight, the last sentence follows naturally as an example of how credibility varies with the reader: "A scientist, for example, would welcome a statement of alternative views." And so again, the original and the revision:

ORIGINAL

A piece of prose may be considered sincere if, in some manner, it establishes its credibility to its audience. The degree of sincerity, however, is relative to the type of person reading it. A logical scientific person would feel gratified if the author included the relationship of counterpoints to his message. To them this technique shows that the author considered opposing viewpoints while presenting his own; an analytical ideal for such an audience.

REVISION

Prose will seem sincere if it seems credible, but how credible will depend on who reads it. A scientist, for example, would welcome a candid statement of alternative views.

I've inserted "candid" both because it clarifies the credibility issue we've just brought into focus, and because the rhythm needs another beat or two here, a kind of adjectival rest before the stressed "statement of alternative views." This back pressure of rhythm on sense illustrates in little just what the whole passage does in large. Thought and style feed back on one another continually as you revise prose. Leaning on rhythm means leaning on thought, and vice versa. And the process never ends.

We've taken this passage about as far as it will go, but one problem still remains. The rhythm seems okay (try it, as always, by reading it aloud with emphasis and coloration), but both sentences run to about the same length. For this reason, the one that follows this passage ought to be either much longer or very short.

When prose is read aloud, sentence shape presents few problems. The voice can shape and punctuate as it goes along. But when the voice atrophies, the eye does not make the same demands with equal insistence, and the larger shaping rhythms that build through a paragraph tend to blur. A problem hard to see and hard to remedy. Consider this passage from a recent popular article by an American economist.

21

A third advantage of the market as a means of social organization is its "devil-take-the-hindmost" approach to questions of individual equity. At first blush this is an outrageous statement worthy of the coldest heart among the nineteenth-century Benthamites. And obviously I have stated the point in a way more designed to catch the eye than to be precise.

In any except a completely stagnant society, an efficient use of resources requires constant change. Consumer tastes, production technologies, locational advantages, and resource availabilities are always in flux. From the standpoint of static efficiency, the more completely and rapidly the economy shifts production to meet changes in tastes, resource availability or locational advantages, the greater the efficiency. From a dynamic standpoint, the greater the advances in technology and the faster they're adopted, the greater the efficiency. While these changes on balance generate gains for society in the form of higher living standards, almost every one of them causes a loss of income to some firms and individuals, often temporary and for only a few, but sometimes long-lasting and for large numbers.

What do you notice? Well, that first sentence, for a start—an almost perfect Normative Undergraduate Sentence, though now from a high government official:

A third advantage
    of the market
    as a means
    of social organization
    is
    its "devil-take-the-hindmost" approach
    to questions
    of individual equity.

Although the sentences do not run to an exact length, they are mostly long and mostly monotonous. No short sentences mean no large-scale emphasis, no climax and finality. The last sentence of paragraph two, though much shorter than any other, doesn't summarize anything. How to supply some shape? For a start, get the lard out of the first paragraph:

A third advantage of the market as a means of social organization is its "devil-take-the-hindmost" approach to questions of individual equity. At first blush this is an outrageous statement worthy of the coldest heart, among the nineteenth-century Benthamites. And obviously I have stated the point in a way more designed to catch the eye than to be precise.

What has been done? I've made one assumption the writer did not, that the audience knows "Benthamite" means "nineteenth century." Otherwise, only fat has been removed. The rhythm has picked up a little. The first sentence now begins more quickly and it has a real verb (though "rests" may not be ideal—how about "remains" or "stands"?). Phrases such as "questions of," "problems of," and "factors of" are simply mindless fillers, bad habits like "like" and "you know" after every third word. An unqualified substantive, paradoxically, almost always comes across stronger. The changes in the second sentence all aim to increase the emphasis on "outrageous statement." In the third, I've tried to underscore the parallelism of "stated the point" and "catch the eye."

The original and revision so far:

ORIGINAL

A third advantage of the market as a means of social organization is its "devil-take-the-hindmost" approach to questions of individual equity. At first blush this is an outrageous statement worthy of the coldest heart among the nineteenth-century Benthamites. And obviously I have stated the point in a way more designed to catch the eye than to be precise.

REVISION

The market's third advantage as a social organization rests in its "devil-take-the-hindmost" approach to individual equity. This outrageous statement seems, at first blush, worthy of the coldest Benthamite heart. And obviously I have stated the point to catch the eye. (LF 33%)

Sentence lengths of 19–13–11 instead of 24–18–20. The result may still fall short of Keats, but at least a decreasing length pattern has begun to form and the last sentence has a bit of zip. Sometimes little changes take you a long way:

~~In any~~ $\stackrel{E}{\cancel{E}}$xcept a $\stackrel{in}{\land}$ ~~completely~~ stagnant society, ~~an~~ efficient use of resources requires constant change.

Again, the adverbial intensifier ("completely") weakens instead of strengthens. And we want to get to "stagnant society" more quickly. Read the two versions aloud several times. Does the revision succeed in placing more stress on "constant change"? The same desire for end-stress now changes "are always in flux" to "always change" in the next sentence. And again in the following one:

$\stackrel{For}{}$ ~~From the standpoint of~~ static efficiency, the more ~~completely and~~ rapidly the economy shifts production to meet change$\stackrel{ing}{\cancel{s in}}$ taste$\stackrel{s}{\land}$, resource$\stackrel{s}{\land}$ ~~availability~~, or locational advantages the $\stackrel{better}{\cancel{greater the efficiency}}$. [And couldn't we say "locations" rather than "locational advantages"?]

24

Now we want to preserve the static/dynamic contrast he is developing—"for static efficiency/for dynamic efficiency":

~~From a~~ dynamic ~~standpoint~~, the ~~greater~~ the ~~advances in technology and the faster they are adopted~~, the ~~greater the efficiency~~.

(handwritten: For efficiency faster / technological change / better)

The two sentences still end with the same phrase, but since they connect more closely the prose no longer sounds like a list or catalogue.

The curse of academic writing, again, is spelling everything out. Academics prepare an assertion the way a cook prepares abalone, by beating it repeatedly with a hammer to make it tender. So in the previous sentence, and in the one that follows:

While these changes ~~on balance~~ generate ~~gains for society in the form of~~ higher living standards, almost ~~every one of them causes a loss of~~ income ~~to some firms and individuals~~ often temporarily and for ~~only~~ a few, but sometimes ~~long lasting~~ and for ~~larger numbers~~. (LF 50%)

(handwritten: all / decrease / permanently many)

The sense may require "on balance," but the rest is pure lard. Again, the ending parallelism is stressed:

temporarily and for a few
permanently and for many.

Our revision so far, then, reads like this:

The market's third advantage as a social organization rests in its "devil-take-the-hindmost" approach to individual equity. This outrageous statement seems, at first blush,

25

worthy of the coldest Benthamite heart. And obviously I have stated the point to catch the eye.

Except in a stagnant society, efficient use of resources requires constant change. For static efficiency, the more rapidly the economy shifts production to meet changing tastes, resources, or locations, the better. For dynamic efficiency, the faster the technological change, the better. While these changes generate higher living standards, almost all decrease income, often temporarily and for a few, but sometimes permanently and for many. (LF 42%)

Sentence length varies enough to stave off monotony and to support, even if it does not specifically illuminate, the argument. Something like a climactic structure has emerged from the second paragraph. I didn't st.ive for this. After you've squeezed out the lard, it emerges by itself.

Here is a final instance of how shape and voice interact. In the original version, the student has written a prose that considers neither the eye nor the ear. You can make sense of it, but it doesn't give you any help. Try reading it aloud.

ORIGINAL

As the cults expose one imposing aspect of the Southern Californian culture, the eminence and glamour of Hollywood reveal an essential part of the city and reflect an important character flaw in the people. The escapist nature of the people manifests itself through an examination of the influence of Hollywood on the inhabitants. The myth and prestige of Hollywood has been a vital instrument in attracting outsiders into the Los Angeles scene. The people that migrate into this region as a result of their dreams regarding Hollywood demonstrate a disillusionment with society.

What's he been smoking? The style stands at ludicrous odds with the subject, an Official Style describing a very unofficial

Southern California; the comedy factor looms larger even than the lard factor. We'll take the revision sentence-by-sentence:

ORIGINAL

As the cults expose one imposing aspect of the Southern Californian culture, the eminence and glamour of Hollywood reveal an essential part of the city and reflect an important character flaw in the people.

Where is the *root action* here? And who, or what, is doing it? The Official Style has taught this student that such things don't really matter. The sentence "sounds okay" after all, doesn't it? Mature and scholarly? If "imposing" jars your ears so soon after "expose," makes you think the two words must be somehow connected in meaning, just shut your eyes and ears as the Official Style recommends. And follow its advice about the verbs, too, by splitting the action into two verbs that mean the same thing: "expose" and "reveal." We'll use just one in the revision, and position it to make the action stand out.

REVISION

Religious cults reveal one part of Southern California culture, Hollywood glamour quite another.

The next sentence shows perfectly how the shopping bag formula blurs the action. Let me highlight with italics all the incipient actions:

The *escapist* nature of the people *manifests* itself through an *examination* of the *influence* of Hollywood on the inhabitants.

The formula provides an excuse to stop thinking in mid-problem. Who is *examining? Influencing?* You cannot tell what

27

this sentence means unless you read the rest of the passage. A quick revision will focus the problem:

ORIGINAL

The myth and prestige of Hollywood has been a vital instrument in attracting outsiders into the Los Angeles scene. The people that migrate into this region as a result of their dreams regarding Hollywood demonstrate a disillusionment with society.

REVISION

Hollywood has attracted a lot of disillusioned people.

Once we see this meaning, the hopelessly confused causality of the puzzling sentence ("The escapist nature . . .") stands out even more. You don't need that sentence at all, of course, but since it is there, let's look at it further. Notice the magnitude of the error it embodies.

The escapist nature of the people manifests itself through an examination of the influence of Hollywood on the inhabitants.

Cause and effect have been reversed, for a start. The "escapist nature manifests itself through an examination" really means that the "examination reveals the escapist nature." The action flows in the opposite direction. The writer goes on to say that Hollywood attracts a lot of disillusioned people from elsewhere. Again the direction of causality has been reversed: they are influencing Hollywood, not being influenced by it. I am beating this dead sentence to make a vital point: when you reverse cause and effect, *you are making a big mistake*. Imagine a military historian saying not "The tank revolutionized infantry warfare" but "Infantry warfare revolutionized the tank." Or an American historian who, instead of "Electricity liberated the farm housewife," wrote "The farm housewife liberated electricity." Yet our chronicler of Hollywood doesn't even know this mistake has been made. A prisoner of the Official Style, he or she just goes on because it fits the formula, "sounds right," and, oh frabjous day, generates a lot of words in a long line of strings of prepositional phrases of various types in the Official Style of writing used in academic departments in universities of higher learning in the United States of America.

I've used reading aloud in this book as the simplest kind of diagnostic tool. It slows you down, makes you read with care instead of speed-reading the prose out of focus, as the Official Style encourages you to do. Reading aloud and with care, and several times, makes prose opaque rather than transparent, makes you look at the words rather than through them to a meaning glimpsed hastily in passing. With this technique in mind, we can now add two more diagnostic procedures to our Paramedic Method:

1. Circle the prepositions.
2. Circle the "is" forms.
3. Ask, "Who is kicking who?"
4. Put this "kicking" action in a simple (not compound) active verb.
5. Start fast—no mindless introductions.
6. Write out the sentence on a blank sheet of paper and look at its shape.
7. Read the sentence aloud with emphasis and feeling.

With this expanded diagnostic repertoire, we'll go on to consider sentence sound and rhythm in more detail in the following chapter.

CHAPTER 3

Sentence Length, Rhythm, and Sound

The elements of prose style—grammar, syntax, shape, rhythm, emphasis, level, usage, and so on—all work as dependent variables. Change one and, to some extent, you change the rest. Rhythm and sound seem, for most prose writers, the most dependent of all. They affect nothing and everything affects them. They do affect something, though. They affect us. Rhythm constitutes the most vital of prose's vital life-signs. Rhythmless, unemphatic prose always indicates that something has gone wrong. And Tin Ears, insensitivity to the sound of words, indicate that the hearing that registers rhythm has been turned off.

Tin Ears have become so common that often you can't tell mistakes from mindlessness. A flack for the army writes:

> Like any new departure in motivating men, the path to a Modern Volunteer Army is beset with perils and pitfalls but it also has potential for progress.

Is the alliteration of "*m*otivating *m*en," "*p*erils and *p*itfalls," "*p*otential for *p*rogress" intended or accidental? It works, at all events, obvious though it may be. The three central

31

phrases of the sentence are spotlighted by an alliterated pair of words, and the last two pairs are put into almost visual contrast:

perils and pitfalls
potential for progress

And "motivating men" finds an alliterative echo in "Modern" while the *p* alliteration has a pre-echo in "path." All this seems to indicate premeditation and a heavy hand. But the writer obviously creates a specific shape and rhythm.

A student happens upon the same kind of sound pattern unintentionally: "Survival supersedes [sic] philosophy, as any passifist [sic] who had to protect himself or his woman knows." Overlooking the spelling and sexism, we still notice that "Survival supercedes pacifist himself his knows" string of "S" sounds. Yet the pattern, a little shorter and less pronounced, might work very well: "Survival supercedes philosophy, as any threatened pacifist soon learns." I'm not sure we can save the following variation on a theme of "P" though: "As man's hopes for perpetuity fall into paradox and collapse under scrutiny, apocalypse dissolves his perplexity." Writing like this testifies to atrophied hearing. Reading it aloud just once would foreground the "Peter Piper" tongue-twisting pattern. And the "formal–informal–informs" jangle from this Poli-Sci paper would highlight itself too: "Acheson's diction, combining formal and informal words, informs the reader." The most typical sound jangle in the Official Style comes from the repetition of "-tion" ("shun") words, as here: "We seek the key through recognition and rejection of arbitrary limitations placed on our potential."

When the ear atrophies, any hope of colloquial emphasis or climax goes up the spout. Look at this flawed diamond: "There is not a sign of life in the whole damned paper (with the possible exception of line 72)." A cinch to fix. Just reverse the order. "With the possible exception of line 72, there is not a sign of life in the whole damned paper." Terrific! I've read papers for hours at a stretch and not come across a sentence so good. Another wasted opportunity: "The more factors the writer meets, the more convincing the article." The shape and rhythm work beautifully. Just substitute a real word for the Official Style slug-word "factor" and everything smiles: "The more nitwits the writer meets, the more convincing the article." Students do sometimes get it right the first time: "People get sick; doctors are needed. Laws are broken; lawyers are needed. Merchandise is sold; businessmen are needed." Beautiful! The same closing pattern—"needed"— for all three; a varied opening one—people/doctors, laws/ lawyers, merchandise/businessmen.

The Official Style formula dries up the human voice, as in this sentence from a drama paper:

ORIGINAL

The first reason acting is rewarding is the chance of being someone else.

The revision encourages the voice to fall on "be someone else."

REVISION

Above all, acting allows us to be someone else for a while.

I've added "for a while" simply to amplify the stress on "be someone else." Try the sentence with and without it. See what I mean?

Sometimes you can see student writing change abruptly from a colloquial voice to an Official Style one: "This point just emphasizes the need of repeated experience for properly utilizing the various sense modalities." The sentence breaks in half after "experience." We expect a finish like, "to use all the senses," and get instead an Official Style translation. Here is a grown-up scholar doing the same thing, this time from

33

sentence to sentence: [Official Style] "The establishment of an error detection mechanism is necessary to establish a sense of independence in our own movement planning and correction. [Gear Change] Unless we know we are doing something wrong, we can't correct it." Change-ups like this just emphasize the voicelessness of the Official Style.

Here is a geography paper that puts sound and rhythm together in a combination wholly alien to the Official Style:

> Twice daily, at sunrise and sunset, a noisy, smokeridden train charges into the stillness of the Arabian desert. Winding about the everchanging windblown sand dunes, the "Denver Zeppler" not only defies the fatal forces of the notorious deserts, but for the nonnative, offers an extraordinary encounter with the tightly closed Saudi society.

The "s" assonance—sunrise, sunset, noisy, smokeridden, stillness—seems to work, and so does "fatal forces." And the sentence allows the voice a full tonal range, a chance for pitch to rise and fall, and a chance to build a climax on "tightly closed Saudi society" as well.

I'm trying to make you self-conscious about the sound of words. Once your ears have had their consciousness raised, they'll catch the easy problems as they flow from the pen— "however clever" will become "however shrewd" in the first draft—and the harder ones will seem easier to revise.

Here *is* a pair of ears whose consciousness badly needs raising. Try reading the passage aloud and with emphasis. Act as if the passage really said something important (what would happen to the sound if I had written "significant" here, instead of "important"?).

> Having shown the applicability of analysis of covariance in straightforward research situations, I shall go on to indicate how several other important methodological top-

ics can be profitably conceptualized as isomorphic in logical structure to the general linear model. . . . For several other topics as well, notably the ecological correlation fallacy, the study of compositional effects, the construction of a "standardized" index, and even the percentaging of cross tables, the logic of linear models is useful. . . .

In regression analysis, as in analysis of variance, if the normality of errors assumption is made, one can analyze the variance due to the explanatory variables, ascertain its significance, and proceed in the same manner as indicated for the analysis of variance situation, and can also test hypotheses about specific values of the parameters.

Reading something like this with emphasis gives you the giggles. Maybe the subject simply repels any shape or rhythm. If the author had written, "Having shown how covariance analysis fits straightforward research problems, I'll now show how it fits some methodological problems," maybe scientific rigor would have been compromised. But whatever it means, your prose ought not read like a laundry list. Prose like this has become generally unreadable, has lost a whole dimension of expressibility. Notice how many polysyllabic words he uses: *applicability, analysis, covariance, straightforward, methodological, profitably, conceptualized, isomorphic, ecological correlation fallacy*. And the sentences are all about the same length.

Sometimes it is good practice to try revising a passage even if you are not sure what it means. You may begin to understand the special terms just by trying to fathom their relationship to one another. Try out such a "naive analysis" here. Here's the full form of the Paramedic Method to help:

1. Circle the prepositions.
2. Circle the "is" forms.
3. Ask "Who is kicking who?"

35

4. Put this "kicking" action in a simple (not compound) active verb.
5. Start fast—no mindless introductions.
6. Write out each sentence on a blank sheet of paper and mark off its basic rhythmic units with a "/."
7. Mark off sentence lengths in the passage with a "/."
8. Read the passage aloud with emphasis and feeling.

The prose problem stands as before. The prepositional phrases encourage a spontaneous monotony. The sentences seem to come in two- or three-line units or five- or six-line units. Using the PM, aim for an LF of 50%, for an emphatic short sentence or two, and for the simplest active, transitive verbs. You might begin: "Analyzing covariance, then, works well in straightforward research situations. It seems to work for other topics as well. . . ."

Sentence length is one of the easiest PM tests to apply. Take a piece of your prose and a red pencil and draw a slash after every sentence. Two or three pages ought to make a large enough sample. If the red marks occur at regular intervals, you have, as they used to say in the White House, a problem. You can chart the problem another way, if you like. Choose a standard length for one sentence and then do a bar graph. If it looks like this,

dandy. If like this,

_____
_____
_____
_____
_____
_____

not so dandy. Obviously, no absolute quantitative standards exist for how much variety is good, how little bad, but the principle couldn't be easier. Vary your sentence lengths. Naturally enough, complex patterns will fall into long sentences and emphatic conclusions work well when short. But no rules prevail except to avoid monotony.

Here's an excerpt from a graduate paper in psychology. I'll mark the sentence lengths off with a "/".

The second class of what is learned is the invariance that defines events, the part of an event that is constant. / Turvey (1977), Pittenger and Shaw (1975), and Shaw and Pittenger (1977) have used this idea to delineate two different kinds of invariants. / For example, one can recognize running no matter who is doing it (transformational invariant), and one can recognize a person no matter what they are doing (structural invariant). / Distinctive features are the basis for the differentiation of objects and motions which can then be seen as invariant when they are, indeed, constant over time. / The third class of what is learned is "higher-order structure." / Distinctive features and the invariance in events belong to hierarchies of increasing abstractness. / For example, there are distinctive features that define sets of things, sets of sets, and so forth. / This aspect of perception relates to processes involved in categorization where a hierarchic organization is the structure of the categorization. /

37

Let's see how it looks on a bar graph:

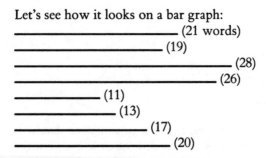

The sentences tend to be long but the variation in length doesn't look too bad from the graph. Alas, nothing is made of it in the prose. Short sentences, especially after long ones, make for climax. At least they can. Here, though, the opportunity drifts by unused. The prose remains wallboard prose; the decision to cut it here rather than there an arbitrary one. Try a revision whose varied sentence length reflects and underlines the meaning.

Measuring sentence length only works in connection with other stylistic variables. Here's an instance where they do work together, a description of the Kennedy inauguration by a professional historian:

It all began in the cold.

It had been cold all week in Washington. / Then early Thursday afternoon the snow came. / The winds blew in icy, stinging gusts and whipped the snow down the frigid streets. / Washingtonians do not know how to drive in the snow: they slide and skid and spin their wheels in panic. / By six o'clock traffic had stopped all over town. / People abandoned their cars in snowdrifts and marched grimly into the gale, heads down, newspapers wrapped around necks and stuffed under coats. / And still the snow fell and the winds blew. /

38

Here's the bar graph:

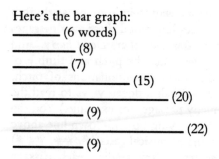

As a rule, much shorter sentences than the first passage. You feel this immediately. Then, too, a more varied sentence length. And the short sentences, especially the beginning one, are strategically placed. Three short ones at the beginning, one in the middle ("By six o'clock"), and one at the end.

The sentence length alternation forms part of a larger rhythmic pattern. Notice the patterns of repetition?

It all began in the cold
    It had been cold

       the snow came . . . The winds blew
And still the snow fell and the winds blew

they slide
   and skid
   and spin

newspapers wrapped around necks
    and stuffed under coats

An occasional assonance pattern ("grimly into the gale," "all week in Washington," "snow . . . frigid streets") helps create discrete rhythmic subpatterns.

39

I've not found a satisfactory way to indicate prose rhythm in a printed book. But try reading aloud these two passages we've just examined, one after the other. *Don't hurry.* And don't read them in a *monotone.* Let the pitch and timbre of your voice vary. Try out various combinations of pitch, stress, and timing. (There are half a dozen ways to read the first sentence of the Kennedy passage, for example.) You can mark pitch variation with a waving up-and-down line above the text, for a start. And mark musical rests (#, ##, ###) after each phrase and sentence. Try reading each passage aloud and having someone else time you, observe where you pause and for how long. The second passage projects a recognizable voice; it is literally "readable." The first passage, academic prose at its most voiceless, is obviously meant to be read—skimmed—silently.

Prose varies widely in the kind of performance instructions that it gives. Official Style academic prose gives very few such instructions. The voice has nowhere to go, no natural place to rise and fall, hurry and pause. Metronome prose: tick, tock, tick, tock, tick, tock.

Here is a prose that offers lots of performance instructions. A sociology professor has taped a hippie-guru telling us what it was like up at Big Sur in the sixties. Try marking the performance instructions; underline, double underline, use quotation marks, whatever.

> When I first got up there, it was a real romantic kind of picture. Man, it was kind of foggy. There were those really beautiful people—men, women, kids, dogs and cats, and campfires. It seemed quiet and stable. And I really felt like love was about me. I thought, "This is the place, man. It was happening. I don't have to do it. I would just kind of fit in and do my thing and that would be like a groove."
>
> After we were there about fifteen or twenty minutes, I heard the people bitching and moaning. I listened to it for awhile and circulated around to hear more about it, and,

man, I couldn't believe it. Here they were secure in their land—beautiful land, where they could be free—and all these people were doing was bitching and moaning. I thought, "Oh, shit, man! Do I have to go into this kind of shit again where I gotta step in and get heavy and get ratty and get people to start talking? Do I have to get them to be open and get in some dialogue and get some communication going and organization? What the —— is wrong with the leadership here, that this kind of state of affairs is happening? And why do I have to do it again? Man, I'm through with it. I just got through with hepatitis and double pneumonia and . . . —— it!" Then I really felt bad.

(Lewis Yablonsky, *The Hippie Trip* [New York: Pegasus, 1968], p. 91.)

This is speech, for a start. And hippie speech, heavily syncopated speech, sliding quickly over interim syllables from heavy stress to heavy stress: "first," "romantic," "foggy," "really," "love." Once you know the syncopated pattern, it is easy to mark up a passage like this. But if you don't know the pattern? Imagine yourself a foreigner trying to read this passage with a natural emphasis. It does sometimes give clues. "This is the *place, man*. It was *happening. I* don't have to do it." The arrangement of the words underscores the sense— the scene has become the actor and the actor the scene. So, too, the alliterative repetition of "go into," "gotta step in," "get heavy," "get ratty," "get people," gives us a clear performance clue. But the passage by itself does not include a full guide to its performance.

How *can* prose include such a guide? It does so often by patterns of repetition, balance, antithesis, and parallelism. The following example comes from Lord Brougham (1778– 1868), a famous Parliamentary orator, in his speech defending Queen Caroline in the divorce proceedings George IV had brought against her. This kind of prose seems fulsome to us, but notice how many performance clues it contains.

41

But, my lords, I am not reduced to this painful necessity. I feel that if I were to touch this branch of the case now, until any event shall afterwards show that unhappily I am deceiving myself—I feel that if I were now to approach the great subject of recrimination, I should seem to give up the higher ground of innocence on which I rest my cause; I should seem to be justifying when I plead Not Guilty; I should seem to argue in extenuation and in palliation of offences, or levities, or improprieties, the least and the lightest of which I stand here utterly to deny. For it is false, as has been said—it is foul and false as those have dared to say, who, pretending to discharge the higher duties to God, have shown that they know not the first of those duties to their fellow-creatures—it is foul, and false, and scandalous in those who have said (and they know that it is so who have dared to say) that there are improprieties admitted in the conduct of the Queen. I deny that the admission has been made. I contend that the evidence does not prove them. I will show you that the evidence disproves them. One admission, doubtless, I do make; and let my learned friends who are of counsel for the Bill take all the benefit of it, for it is all that they have proved by their evidence.

Several powerful variables contend in a prose like this. The patterning aims above all to establish a tone of high seriousness. But look at it simply for performance clues. It tells us exactly how it ought to be performed. Shape and sound coincide. It builds to a climactic central assertion and then tapers off. Perhaps a diagram will help:

But, my lords,
I am not reduced to this painful necessity.
I feel that if
I were to touch this branch of the case now, until

any event shall afterwards show that unhappily
I am deceiving myself—
I feel that if
I were now to approach the great subject of
        recrimination,
I should seem to give up the higher ground of
        innocence on which
I rest my cause;
I should seem to be justifying when
I plead Not Guilty;
I should seem to argue in extenuation
        and in palliation of
        offences, or improprieties,
        the least and
        the lightest of which
I stand here utterly to deny.
        For it is false, as has been said
         it is foul and false as those have dared to say
      who pretending to discharge
      the high duties of God
have shown that they know not
      the first of those duties to their fellow men
it is foul, and false, and scandalous
        in those who have said
      (and they know that it is so
        who have dared to say)
THAT THERE ARE IMPROPRIETIES ADMITTED IN THE
        CONDUCT OF THE QUEEN
I deny that the admission has been made;
I contend that the evidence does not prove them;
I will show you that the evidence disproves them.
One admission, doubtless, I do make
    and let my learned friends who are
      of counsel for the Bill
Take *all* the benefit of *it,* for *it* is *all* that they have
            proved by their evidence.

Notice how the conclusion is handled? He uses a chiasmus (an *ab:ba* pattern) to fold the last clause back up upon itself and then uses the last prepositional phrase to end the whole rhythmic unit. And the main pattern stands clear. First a series of repetitive hammer-blow assertions; next a set of balanced assertions and rebuttals; then the central point; then a short return to the first pattern and a short return to the second; then the final chiasmus.

We don't write prose like this anymore, but whether you relish it as I do or not, you ought to try in your own writing to give equally good performance instructions. For, again, that is what sentence length, rhythm, and sound are—a series of instructions for how your sentence should be performed. And if your reader takes pleasure in performing your prose, you have her on your side. She is acting in your play.

We've seen how sentences become shapeless when the voice goes out of them. Prose that is not *voiced* becomes shapeless and unemphatic in the same way that an unexercised muscle loses its tone. And it works the other way, too. If we do not look *at* a piece of prose, try to perform it, we'll cease to hear real voices, our own and others, when we speak. Writing and speaking form a spiral. If they intensify each other, the spiral goes up. If they don't, each drives the other down.

CHAPTER 4

The Official Style

Up to now we've been analyzing particular stylistic elements—shape, rhythm, emphasis. We've seen, in the process, that these elements are interrelated, that they seem to proceed from the same aesthetic, that they constitute a common style. In the examples we've been revising, we've been in effect translating from the Official Style into plain English. Now we are going to do this directly, focus on the Official Style as an exercise in stylistic analysis and translation. At the same time, we'll try, instead of simply condemning the Official Style, to ask how and why it has come about, how it works in the world.

Students of style have traditionally distinguished three basic levels—high, middle, low. The content of these categories varied somewhat, but usually the high style was a formal and ornamental style for a solemn and ritualized occasion, the low style was the loose and sloppy intercourse of daily life, and the middle style stood somewhere in between. Since World War II, American prose has worked a pronounced variation on this enduring pattern.

The low style of ordinary conversation seems to have disintegrated into the series of "I mean," "Like—you know?" "So I go and then she goes" spastic tics with which—or through which—American undergraduates talk to one another. And since we have come to suspect both fancy language and formal ceremony in America, we have come to suspect the high style, too. As a substitute, we've clasped to our bosoms the Official Style. The Official Style is often stigmatized as bureaucratese or jargon and often is both. But it is a genuine style, and one that reflects the genuine bureaucratization of American life. It has its own rules and its own reasons, and anyone writing prose nowadays in America must come to know both. The Official Style runs from school days to retirement. As soon as you realize that you live "in a system," whether P.S. 41, the University of California, or the Department of Agriculture, you start developing the Official Style. Used unthinkingly, it provides the quickest tip-off that you have become system-sick, and look at life only through the system's eyes. It is a scribal style, ritualized, formulaic, using a private vocabulary to describe a particular kind of world. And it is, increasingly, the only kind of prose style America ever sees. It is also, along with the social changes that sponsor it, the main reason for our prose problem. The low style has dissolved, the high style has hardened and dehydrated, and the middle style has simply evaporated. The Official Style threatens to replace all three.

If you can analyze, write, and translate it, maybe you can find your niche in the System without losing your soul to it. For you may have to write in the Official Style but you don't have to think in it. If you are the first on the scene after the car has missed the curve, climbed the hedge and ended up on your lawn, you won't ask the driver, as did the policeman, "How,uh, did you achieve this configuration?"

Sometimes you can see the Official Style seizing its prey like a boa constrictor and gradually squeezing the life out of it. Here's a student feeling its grip.

> Twelve-year-old boys like to fight. Consequently, on several occasions I explained to them the negative aspects of fighting. Other responsibilities included keeping them dry (when near the creek or at times of rain), seeing that they

bathed, attending to any minor wounds they acquired, and controlling their mischievous behavior. Another responsibility was remaining patient with the children.

The first sentence says simply what it has to say. The second sentence starts to sound like a report. It strives for a needless explicitness ("on several occasions") and it aims for a pseudo-scientific neutrality of description, "the negative aspects of fighting." To remain on the same stylistic level as the first sentence, it ought to read. "So, I often told them to stop." "Other responsibilities included" is the language of a job description. The frantic scramble of a summer camp is being viewed through a personnel form. The prose is scary as well as stilted because life has been reduced to something that will fit in a file cabinet. Only on official forms do small boys "acquire minor wounds" or counselors "attend" them. In life, they cut themselves and you give them a Band-Aid. In life, you keep them out of the creek and out of the rain, instead of "keeping them dry (when near the creek or at times of rain)." And, instead of "controlling their mischievous behavior," you make them behave or even give them a kick in the pants. As for "Another responsibility was remaining patient with the children," that translates into, "I had to keep my temper." If the writer had stayed on the level he began with, he would have written:

> Twelve-year-old boys like to fight. Often, I had to stop them. And I had to keep them out of the rain, and the creek, and mischief generally. I had to give out Band-Aids and keep my temper.

Why didn't he? You don't write the Official Style by nature. It has to be learned. Why did he fall into it here? He was applying for something. And you apply for something—in this case, admission to medical school—on a form. And a form requires an official style. The Official Style. It makes

47

what you've done sound important and, still more important than important, *official*.

Ever since George Orwell's famous essay "Politics and the English Language" (1946), the Official Style has been interpreted as a vast conspiracy to soften our minds and corrupt our political judgment. Social science jargon has been seen as pure hokum, an attempt to seem more scientific than you are. And the language of the Pentagon bureaucrats during the Vietnam War often seemed to combine the worst of these two worlds. The Orwell conspiracy theory is sometimes true, but not the whole truth. We all want to fit in, to talk the language of the country. This desire is what keeps society glued together. So the impulses that attract us to the Official Style are not always perverse or depraved. Just the opposite. They are the primary social impulses. And so when we analyze the Official Style, we're really talking about how we live now, about our *society* as well as our prose, about how to survive in the System. What does the prose tell us about the society?

Well, it is a euphemistic society, for a start. It thinks of every town dump as a "Sanitary Landfill Site," every mentally retarded child as "exceptional," every dog catcher as an "animal welfare officer." Society may have its pains and problems, but language can surgarcoat them.

The second rule in this society is "Keep your head down. Don't assert anything you'll have to take the blame for. Don't, if you can help it, assert anything at all." Anthony Sampson has culled a few examples of this super-caution from a British Civil Service version of the Official Style and supplied plain language translations.

We hope that it is fully appreciated that . . .
    You completely fail to realize that . . .

Greater emphasis should be laid on . . .
    You haven't bothered to notice . . .

We have the impression that insufficient study has been given to . . .
    No one has considered . . .

Our enquiry seemed to provide a welcome opportunity for discussions of problems of this kind . . .
    No one had thought of that before . . .

We do not think that there is sufficient awareness . . .
    There is ignorance . . .

There has been a tendency in the past to overestimate the possibilities of useful short-term action in public investment . . .
    You should look ahead . . .

There should be an improvement in the arrangements to enable ministers to discharge their collective responsibility . . .
    The cabinet should work together . . .

(Anatomy of Britain, New York: Harper & Row, 1962)

The main rule is clear. Don't make an assertion you can get tagged with later. It may come back to haunt you. So never write "I think" or "I did." Keep the verbs passive and impersonal: "It was concluded that" or "appropriate action was initiated on the basis of systematic discussion indicating that." Often, as with politicians being interviewed on TV, the Official Style aims deliberately at saying nothing at all, but saying it in the required way. Or at saying the obvious in a seemingly impressive way. The Official Stylist seems in control of everything but responsible for nothing. Thus a congressman, instead of saying that the government will listen to consumer complaints, says that it will "review existing mechanisms of consumer input, thruput, and output and seek ways of improving these linkages via consumer consumption channels." The computer language of input, output, and interface has been seized upon by the Official Style as a kind of poetic diction, a body of sacred and intrinsically beautiful metaphors. Thus, a U.S. senator indicted on bribery charges does not ask the advice of his friends. He instead is "currently receiving personal and political input from my supporters and friends throughout the state."

It is often hard to tell with the Official Style how much is self-conscious put-on and how much is real ineptitude, genuine system-sickness. Students often say that the length and physical weight of their papers is more important than what they say, yet it is not only in school that papers are graded thus. Here is a famous Washington lawyer, talking about legal language.

> In these days when every other type of professional report, good or poor, is dressed up in a lovely ringed and colored plastic binder, some people still are prone to judge legal performance quantitatively by verbal volume. Thirty years ago two of us answered a difficult and intricate legal problem by concisely writing: "Gentlemen, after examining the statute in your state, all analogous statutes, and all of the cases, we have concluded that what you want to do is lawful." That client was not happy; he went down to Wall Street, got the same opinion backed by thirty turgid typewritten pages, and felt much more comfortable.
>
> (Quoted in Joseph C. Guelden, *The Superlawyers* [New York: Dell, 1972], p. 306)

It is not only schoolteachers who find length and obscurity impressive.

Here is another example of the Official Style, social science dialect:

> A policy decision inexorably enforced upon a depression-prone individual whose posture in respect to his total

50

psychophysical environment is rendered antagonistic by apprehension or by inner-motivated disinclination for on-going participation in human existence is the necessity for effectuating a positive selection between two alternative programs of action, namely, (a) the continuance of the above-mentioned existence irrespective of the dislocations, dissatisfactions, and disabilities incurred in such a mode, or (b) the voluntary termination of such existence by self-initiated instrumentality, irrespective in this instance of the undetermined character of the subsequent environment, if any, in which the subject may be positioned as an end result of this irrevocable determination.

Serious or a joke? A joke. In fact, one of the clever variations on common clichés devised by Richard D. Altick in *A Preface to Critical Reading* to illustrate the Official Style. The text varied is, of course, "To be or not to be, that is the question."

Now, by contrast, someone genuinely system-sick. No joke. He has come to *think* in the Official Style. A librarian, of all people, he is trying to tell us that some books will be kept behind the desk, others put on shelves outside:

> Primarily, this reorganization and the related changes are designed to facilitate the processing of lists. Placing responsibility for the processing of lists directly within the Technical Processing Division will provide a smoother and more efficient work flow, which we anticipate will result in your materials becoming more readily available. Second, it will allow optimum access to the collection, and third, provide a browsing capability formerly denied users of reserved materials.
>
> For this new system to be successful we need your full cooperation. The attached Guidelines for Reserve Lists details the manner in which we need lists prepared. Essentially, we are requesting that required readings be distinguished from optional readings. Required readings stipu-

lated for two-hour use will be placed on closed reserve in an area behind the circulation desk. Required readings circulating for one day will remain in the open stacks; however, as opposed to regular open stack materials, these books will be marked to indicate one day use. Optional readings will circulate for regular loan periods.

In the past, the primary means for soliciting faculty input for acquiring materials for the College Library has been through reserve lists. It is our desire that optimal reading lists for undergraduates will be an effective mechanism for faculty to identify materials for the library's open stack collection.

It is our hope that you will find these changes mutually beneficial for yourselves and your students.

Your cooperation and assistance in this matter will be greatly appreciated.

If he translated this into language less wordy, shapeless, pompous, and pretentious, he might make things clearer to the faculty but he would be only a librarian, not a bureaucratic witch doctor. He would be simply putting the books out on the shelf, not "providing a browsing capability."

You must, if you are to write prose in an America and a world fated to become ever more bureaucratic, learn how to use the Official Style, even perhaps how to enjoy it, without becoming imprisoned by it. You must manage to remember who is on first base, even if often you will not want to let on that you know.

Long ago, La Rochefoucauld talked about a grave manner as "a mysterious carriage of the body to cover defects of the mind." The Official Style has elevated this into an article of faith. Here is a sociological sample collected by Malcolm Cowley, with his translation:

In effect, it was hypothesized, that certain physical data categories including housing types and densities, land use characteristics, and ecological location constitute a scalable content area. This could be called a continuum of residential desirability. Likewise, it was hypothesized that several social data categories, describing the same census tracts, and referring generally to the social stratification system of the city, would also be scalable. This scale would be called a continuum of socio-economic status. Thirdly, it was hypothesized that there would be a high positive correlation between the scale types on each continuum.

Here's the translation:

Rich people live in big houses set farther apart than those of poor people. By looking at an aerial photograph of any American city, we can distinguish the richer from the poorer neighborhoods.

("Sociological Habit Patterns In Linguistic Transmogrification," *The Reporter*, Sept. 20, 1956)

Such prose seems to aim at being scientific but actually wants to be priestly, to cast a witch doctor's spell. To translate the prose into a plain style—that is, to revise it into ordinary English—breaks the spell and defeats the purpose.

We face, then, the euphemistic habit yet again, though on a larger scale. The Official Style always wants to make things seem better than they are, more mysterious and yet somehow more controlled, more inevitable. It strives, at all times, both to disarm and to impress us. It suggests that it sees the world differently—sees, even, a different world. It suggests that those who see in this way form a happy band of brothers. Now such a use of language does not, to students of literature, sound unfamiliar. It is called *poetic diction*. And this is what the Official Style amounts to—poetry. The first rule about poetry is that you cannot translate it into prose without destroying its real meaning. And here we come to the central problem with the Official Style. There is no point in reproaching it for not being clear. It does not want to be clear. It wants to be poetic. It seems to be distant and impersonal, but it really is just the opposite. At its best, it wants to tell you how it *feels* to be an official, to project the sense of numinous self-importance officialdom confers. It wants to make a prosaic world mysterious.

I know, I know. It doesn't do it very well. But that's not the point. Until we see what it is trying to do, we can neither understand it nor translate it with any pleasure. Maybe a comparison will make the point clearer. Here is a little glossary of poetic diction that Alexander Pope compiled for a satire on false poetic sublimity called *Peri Bathos* (1728). He gives first the ordinary language equivalent and then the poetic diction.

> Who knocks at the Door?
> For whom thus rudely pleads my loud-tongued gate
> That he may enter? . . .

> See who is there?
> Advance the fringed curtains of thy eyes,
> And tell me who comes yonder. . . .

> Shut the Door.
> The wooden guardian of our privacy
> Quick on its axle turn. . . .

> Bring my clothes.
> Bring me what Nature, tailor to the *Bear,*
> To *Man* himself denied: She gave me Cold,
> But would not give me Clothes. . . .

> Light the Fire.
> Bring forth some remnant of the *Promethean* theft,
> Quick to expand th' inclement air congealed
> By *Boreas'* rude breath. . . .

Snuff the Candle.
Yon Luminary amputation needs,
Thus shall you save its half-extinguished life.

Uncork the Bottle, and chip the Bread.
Apply thine engine to the spongy door,
Set *Bacchus* from his glassy prison free,
And strip white *Ceres* of her nut-brown coat.

Here is another glossary, an unintentional self-satire this time, issued by the U.S. Office of Education (1971). Again, first the ordinary term and then the poetic diction.

- ACTIVITY—Allocation of personnel and logistic resources to accomplish an identifiable objective. Activities constitute the basis for defining personnel assignments and for scheduling system operations.

- ANALYSIS—The splitting of an entity into its constituent parts, and the determination of relations among the parts and groups of the components.

- DEVELOPMENT—Production and refinement of a system or a product through trial-revision until it accomplishes its specified objectives.

- FUNCTIONS—Those things (actions) that must be done to accomplish the overall job are referred to as functions.

- IMPLEMENT—To carry out. To fulfill. To give practical effect to and ensure of actual fulfillment by concrete measures.

- IMPROVEMENT—Enhanced performance on any important dimension without detriment to the other essential dimensions.

- MISSION—The job to be done, be it a product, a completed service, or a change in the condition of something or somebody.

- NEED—A discrepancy or differential between "what is" and "what should be" (i.e., "what is required" or "what is desired"). In educational planning, "need" refers to problems rather than solutions, to the student "product" rather than to the resources for achieving that product, to the ends of education rather than to the means for attaining those ends.

- OBJECTIVES—That toward which effort is directed. An intent statement and prediction for which a procedure is developed and resources allocated with a specific time frame and a measurable product signaling attainment.

- PLANNING CAPABILITY OR PLANNING COMPETENCE—The organizational, procedural, technological, and support arrangements by which an agency has the capacity to apply problem-solving processes to any problem that it may face.

- TASKS—Elements of a function that, when performed by people and things in proper sequential order, will or should resolve the parent function. Tasks may be performed by people, equipment, or people/equipment combination.

  (Robert A. Watson, "Making Things Perfectly Clear," *Saturday Review*, July 24, 1971)

This bureaucratic glossary was issued in the name of clarity, but aims obviously at something else entirely, at a playful, poetic, ornamental use of language. Those who use the Official Style seldom acknowledge the paradox, but you must learn to see it if you are not to make grotesque mistakes. Clarity is the last thing the Official Style really wants to create and, if you find yourself in a bureaucratic context, the last thing *you* want to create. If you are writing a government report, a paper in sociology, or a grant-proposal in education,

56

writing it in plain English will be disastrous. You may well want, in marshalling your thoughts, to write out an ordinary-language version. But you must then translate it into the Official Style. You must, that is, learn to read, write, and translate the Official Style as if it were a foreign language. Play games with it by all means, but don't get fooled by it.

Bureaucrats have, in the last few years, begun to do just this—play games with it. One government official, Philip Broughton, created something called the "Systematic Buzz Phrase Projector." It consists of three columns of words:

Column 1	Column 2	Column 3
0. integrated	0. management	0. options
1. total	1. organizational	1. flexibility
2. systematized	2. monitored	2. capability
3. parallel	3. reciprocal	3. mobility
4. functional	4. digital	4. programming
5. responsive	5. logistical	5. concept
6. optional	6. transitional	6. time-phase
7. synchronized	7. incremental	7. projection
8. compatible	8. third-genera-	8. hardware
9. balanced	tion	9. contingency
	9. policy	

(*Newsweek,* May 6, 1968)

You think of any three numbers, 747 say, and then read off the corresponding words, "synchronized digital projection." It is a device to generate verbal ornament, a machine for poetic diction. Try making up a version for whatever dialect of the Official Style you need to write—sociological, educational, psychoanalytic. Not only will it lend new resonance and authority to your prose, it will act as a multiplier, increasing length and weight. It also acts as a mechanical muse, generates inspiration. Produce a phrase by the three-number procedure, invent a sentence for it, and then spend a paragraph or two reflecting on what it might mean. Invent a reality to which the phrase can refer.

The basic elements of the Official Style ought by now to stand clear. (1) It is built on *nouns,* vague, general, nouns. These are usually of Latin deriva*tion,* "shun" words like fixa*tion,* devia*tion,* func*tion,* construc*tion,* educa*tion,* organi-za*tion.* (2) These are often, as in the game, modified by adjectives made up from other nouns like them, as in "incremental throughput" or "functional input." (3) All action is passive and impersonal. No active intransitive verbs and no direct objects. Never "I decided to fire him" but "It has been determined that that individual's continued presence in the present personnel configuration would tend to the detriment of the ongoing operational efficiency of the organizational unit in which the individual is currently employed." (4) Nothing is called by its ordinary name. You don't decide to bomb a town; instead, "It has been determined to maintain an aggressive and operational attack posture." You don't set up an office, you "initiate an ongoing administrative facility." (5) The status quo is preserved even in syntax. All motion is converted into stasis. The Official Style denies, as much as possible, the reality of action. You don't dislike someone, you "maintain a posture of disapproval toward" him. You don't decide to hire someone, you "initiate the hiring situation."

These rules should help you to translate into and out of the Official Style when needed. How to know when that "when" has come we'll be considering in the following two chapters.

CHAPTER 5

Why Bother?

I've been arguing that much of the prose problem comes from the cluster of goals and attributes that make up the Official Style. To this degree the paramedic analogy holds and the prose can be revised using simple procedures. We have seen what the Official Style looks like: dominantly a noun style; a concept style; a style whose sentences have no design, no shape, rhythm, or emphasis; an unreadable, voiceless, impersonal style; a style built on euphemism and various kinds of poetic diction; a style with a formulaic structure, "is" plus a string of prepositional phrases before and after. And we've seen how to revise it. A set of do-it-yourself techniques, the Paramedic Method, handles the problem nicely.

But you may well be asking, at this point, "Why bother?" Why try to see in a blind world? There are two answers, or rather two kinds of answers. The first kind: "If you can see and others can't, you'll get ahead." Sometimes this is true and sometimes not. Generally, it helps to write better prose. It makes for a better statement of purpose when you apply for law school or a job. It will probably not, however, get you a better grade on a sociology paper, where plain prose sounds simple-minded or even flip. The sensible procedure here: learn both languages, the plain and the Official Style. The second kind of answer is both simpler than the first and more complex. We've looked at many examples of inept student writing—writing that ranges from shapeless to mindless. The second kind of answer to "Why bother?" is simply, "Are you

59

willing to sign your name to what you have written? To present yourself in public—whether it matters to anyone else or not—as this kind of person?" In a sense, it is a simple question: "Whatever the advantage—or disadvantage—ought I do this?" The primary kind of moral question: If everyone else is committing murder, ought I do the same? Do you choose to encounter the world on its terms or on your own? A simple question but one we must all answer for ourselves. "The style is the man," people often say. Perhaps they mean that to this basic moral question you'll give the same answer for writing as for the rest of your behavior. Yet the question is complex, too, for what kind of behavior is "prose behavior"? Prose is usually described in a moral vocabulary—"sincere," "open" or "devious," and "hypocritical"—but is this vocabulary justified? Why, for that matter, has it been so moralistic? Why do so many people feel that bad prose threatens the foundations of civilization? And why, in fact, do we think "bad" the right word to use for it?

Let's start with the primary ground for morality, the self. We may think of the self as both a dynamic and a static entity. It is static when we think of ourselves as having central, fixed selves independent of our surroundings, an "I" we can remove from society without damage, a central self inside our head. But it becomes dynamic when we think of ourselves as actors playing social roles, a series of roles that vary with the social situation in which we find ourselves. Such a social self amounts to the sum of all the public roles we play. Our complex identity comes from the constant interplay of these two kinds of self. Our final identity is usually a mixed one, few of us being completely the same in all situations or, conversely, social chameleons who change with every context. What allows the self to grow and develop is the free interplay between these two kinds of self. If we were completely sincere we would always say exactly what we think—and cause social chaos. If we were always acting an appropriate role, we would be certifiably insane. Reality, for each of

60

us, presents itself as constant oscillation between these two extremes.

When we say that writing is sincere, we mean that somehow it has managed to express this complex oscillation, this complex self. It has caught the accent of a particular self, a particular mixture of the two selves. Sincerity can't point to any *specific* verbal configuration, of course, since sincerity varies as widely as man himself. The sincere writer has not said exactly what he felt in the first words that occur to him. That might produce a revolutionary tirade, or "like-you-know" conversational babble, or the gross student mistakes we've been reviewing. Nor has a sincere writer simply borrowed a fixed language, as when a bureaucrat writes in the Official Style. He has managed to create a style which, like the social self, can become part of society, can work harmoniously in society and, at the same time, like the central self, can represent his unique selfhood. He holds his two selves in balance; this is what "authority" in prose really means.

Now simply reverse this process. What the act of writing prose involves for the writer is an integration of his self, a deliberate act of balancing its two component parts. It represents an act of socialization, and it is by repeated acts of such socialization that we become sociable beings, that we grow up. Thus, the act of writing models the presentation of self in society, constitutes a rehearsal for social reality. It is not simply a question of a pre-existent self making its message known to a pre-existent society. It is not, initially, a question of message at all. Writing is a way to clarify, strengthen, and energize the self, to render individuality rich, full, and social. This does not mean writing that flows, as Terry Southern immortally put it, "right out of the old guts onto the goddamn paper." Just the opposite. Only by taking the position of the reader toward one's own prose, putting a reader's pressure on it, can the self be made to grow. Writing should enhance and expand the self, allow it to try out new possibilities, tentative selves.

The moral ingredient in writing, then, works first not on the morality of the message but on the nature of the sender, on the complexity of the self. "Why bother?" To invigorate and enrich your selfhood, to increase, in the most literal sense, your self-consciousness. Writing, properly pursued, does not make you better. It makes you more alive. This is why our growing illiteracy ought to distress us. It tells us something, something alarming, about the impoverishment of our selves. We say that we fear written communication will break down. Unlikely. And if it does we can always, as we do anyway, pick up the phone. Something more fundamental is at stake, the self-hood and sociability of the communicators. We are back to the basic peculiarity of *writing*—it is *premeditated* utterance, and in that premeditation lives its first if not its only value. "Why bother?" "To find out who I really am." It is not only what we think that we discover in writing, but what we are and can be.

We can now see why the purely neutral, transparent style is so hard to write and so rare, and why we take to jargon, to the Official Style, to all the varieties of poetic diction, verbal ornament, with such alacrity. We are doing more in writing, any writing, than transmitting neutral messages. We want to convey our feelings about what we say, our attitude toward the human relationships we are thus establishing. Neutral communications do not come naturally to man. What matters most to him is his relationships with his fellow men. These urges continually express themselves through what we write. They energize what we call style. Style has attracted a moralistic vocabulary because it expresses all the patterns of human behavior that morality must control. This moralistic vocabulary leads to a good deal of confusion, but it arises naturally enough from the way human beings use literary style.

How rare a purely neutral human relationship really is you can see simply by reflecting on your daily life. Is there any response, however trivial, that we don't color with hand gestures, facial expressions, postures of the body? Human beings are nonstop expressors, often through minute subconscious clues. We sense, immediately, that a friend is angry at us by the way he says "Hello." He doesn't say, "Go to hell, you skunk" instead of "Hello." He doesn't need to. Tense vocal chords, pursed lips, a curt bob of the head perhaps, do just as well. No one has put a percentage figure to this kind of human communication, but it far outranks plain statement in frequency and importance. The same truth prevails for written communication. We are always trying to say more than we actually do. This voice-over technique is our natural way of speaking.

We can now begin to see what kinds of value judgments make sense about prose and what kinds don't. The prevailing wisdom teaches that the best prose style is the most transparent, the least seen; prose ideally aspires to a perfect neutrality; like the perfect secretary, it gets the job done without intruding. Rare we have seen this ideal to be. But is it even ideal? Doesn't it rule out most of what we call good prose? The ideal document of perfect neutrality would be a laundry list. We mean by good prose something a little different. We mean a style suffused with a sense of human relationships, of specific occasions and why they matter. We mean a style that expresses a genuinely complex and fully socialized self. We've cleared up a lot of muddy student writing up to now. The metaphor "clear up" is clear enough, and there is no reason not to use it, but we can now explain more precisely what we have been doing. An incoherent student style is "clear enough." It depicts clearly an incoherent mind, an incoherent student. Looked at in this way, all prose is clear. What revision aims for is to "clear up" the student, to present a self more coherent, more in control. A mind thinking, not a mind asleep. It aims, that is, not to denature the human relationship the prose sets up, but to enhance and enrich it. It is not trying to squeeze out the expression of personality but to make such expression possible, not trying to squeeze out all record of a particular occasion and its human relationships but to make them maximally clear. Again, this is why we worry so much about bad prose. It signifies incoherent people, failed social relationships. This worry makes sense only if we feel that prose, ideally, should express human relationships and feelings, not abolish them.

Think, for example, about a familiar piece of prose we might all agree to be successful, Lincoln's Gettysburg Address. Its brevity has been much praised, but the brevity does not work in a vacuum. It makes sense, becomes expressive, only in relation to the occasion. Lincoln took for his subject the inevitable gap between words and deeds. At Gettysburg, this gap was enormous, and the shortness of Lincoln's speech symbolizes just this gap. No speech could do justice to what had happened at Gettysburg. Lincoln's brevity did not *remove* the emotion of the occasion but *intensified* it. It did not ignore the occasion's human relationships but celebrated them. We think of it as a monument to brevity and clarity not because it neutralizes human emotion but because it so superbly enshrines just the emotions that fit the occasion.

We might, as a contrasting example, consider a modern instance of public prose. In 1977, the Federal Aviation Administration published a document called *Draft Environmental Impact Statement for the Proposed Public Acquisition of the Existing Hollywood-Burbank Airport*. It discussed, in two volumes and about fifteen hundred pages, the noise and pollution problems the airport caused and what might happen if the Lockheed Corporation sold it to a consortium of interested city governments. The *Statement* also included extensive testimony about the airport by private citizens. The *Statement* itself provides a perfect—if at times incomprehensible—example of the Official Style; the citizens, with some exceptions, speak and write plain English. The *Statement* as a whole thus constitutes an invaluable extended example of how the two styles conflict in real life.

The issue posed was simple. Lockheed was going to shut the airport down and sell the land if the city governments didn't buy it. Would the loss of airport jobs and public transportation be compensated by the increased peace and quiet in the East San Fernando Valley? Horrible noise on the one hand; money on the other. How do you relate them to one another? The different styles in the *Statement* put the problem in different ways. They seem, sometimes, to be describing different problems. Here's a sample of the *Statement's* archetypal Official Style:

The findings of ongoing research have shown that a number of physiological effects occur under conditions of noise exposure. . . . These studies demonstrate that noise exposure does influence bodily changes, such as the so-called vegetative functions, by inhibition of gastric juices, lowered skin resistance, modified pulse rate and increased metabolism. . . .

Other studies have investigated the generalized physiological effects of noise in relation to cardiovascular disturbances, gastrointestinal problems, impairment of performance on motor tracking tasks and vascular disturbances, as well as various physical ailments. Miller (1974) states that, "Steady noise of 90 dB increases tension in all muscles." Welch (1972) concludes that "environmental sound has all-pervasive effects on the body, influencing virtually every organ system and function that has been studied," and Cohen (1971) summarized that "the distressing effects of noise alone or combined with other stress factors can eventually overwhelm man's capability for healthy adjustment with resultant physical or mental ailments." . . .

The VTN survey determined the presence of annoyance reactions which have been identified as indicators of stressful response to environmental noise among respondents both inside and outside the noise impact area. As is re-

65

ported in Section 2.5.3 (Annoyance Reactions as Determinants of Community Response to Airport Noise) of this chapter, individuals' beliefs about the noise and the noise source tend to determine their reactions to its occurrence and the amount of disturbance it creates. . . .

When asked for the three things they liked least about their neighborhood, 14.2 percent of the respondents in the high noise exposure area, compared to only 5.3 percent of those residing in the low noise exposure area, indicated aircraft noise among the three. It appears from these observations that Hollywood-Burbank Airport does produce annoyance reactions among residents of the East Valley, which indicates a perception of environmental stress associated with Airport noise.

No need to do a detailed analysis at this stage of the game—the formula as before. In this distanced and impersonal world, no one ever suffers; they experience "the presence of annoyance reactions." And, in the report's ever-cautious style, it only "appears" that the airport produces such reactions among residents. Later, in the residents' comments, that "appearance" becomes an oppressive reality.

Human beings, we need to remind ourselves here, are social beings. Our reality is a social reality. Our identity draws its felt life from our relation to other people. We become uneasy if, for extended periods of time, we neither hear nor see other people. We feel uneasy with the Official Style for the same reason. It has no human voice, no face, no personality behind it. It creates no society, encourages no social conversation. We feel that it is *unreal*. The "better" it is, the more typical, the more unreal it becomes. And so we can answer the question of whether you can write a "good" Official Style. No. Not unless you want to erase human reality, make the Official Style yet more Official.

But public prose need not erase human reality. It can do just the opposite, as in the following passage from the same

66

report—a letter from a homeowners' group president. With it, we return to human life.

Our Homeowners Association was formed about a year and a half ago principally because of an overwhelming fear of what might happen to our homes, schools and community as a result of any steps which might be taken by Lockheed and/or the City of Burbank. Our community is inexorably linked to Hollywood-Burbank Airport. The northern part of the North/South runway is in our city. . . .

Our community consists of a vast majority of single-family residences, and long-time owners with "paid in full" or "almost paid up" mortgages. We have been told, "You moved in next to the airport, it was there before you were." This is true in most cases. But, and this is a big "but"—it was an entirely different airport when most of us moved into the area. 20 to 25 years ago, the airport was "home" to small planes. We actually enjoyed watching them buzz around, and many of us spent Sunday afternoons at the airport while our children were amused watching the little planes. However, the advent of the jet plane at HBA changed the entire picture. Suddenly we were the neighbors of a Noise Factory! . . .

Our children are bombarded with noise in 2 local elementary schools, Roscoe and Glenwood. Teachers have to stop teaching until the noise passes over and everyone waits "for the next one." If the school audiometrist wants an in-depth test for a child with questionable hearing, the child must be taken away from the school altogether to eliminate outside noises.

Our backyards, streets, parks and churches, too, are inundated with noise . . . noise is an ever-constant fact of life for us. There is seldom a time when one cannot hear a plane somewhere in the vicinity—it may be "up" or it may be "down," but once a motor is turned on, we hear it!

67

We might well be asked, "Why do you continue to live in such a place?" Put in plain and simple terms—we have no place else to go! Years have passed and we have put more money into our mortgages and into our property. We have developed long-time friendships with neighbors and the Community. We don't want to move! . . .

Where do we go? Who is going to pay us—and how much will we be paid—for being uprooted? Who sets the price on losing a street and an entire neighborhood full of long-time friends? If 7 schools are to be closed, where do the children go? What happens to the faculty and staff at the schools? The parochial schools? The small business man who sells consumer goods—what happens when there is no one to sell to?

A living voice! Human society! Plain English, in such a context, takes on the moral grandeur of epic, of the high style. The language of ordinary life reasserts our common humanity. Precisely the humanity, we have now come to see, the Official Style seeks to banish. It is a bad style, then, because it denatures human relations. When we consider that it is becoming the accepted language for the organizations that govern human relations, we can begin to see how stylistic and moral issues converge.

Our current literacy crisis may come, then, from more than inattention, laziness, or even the diabolical purposes of the Official Style. It may come, ultimately, from our meager ideal for prose. We say that what we want is only a serviceable tool—useful, neutral, durable, honest, practical, and so on. But none of us takes such an attitude even toward our tools! If we earn our living with them, we love them. We clean and polish and lubricate them. We prefer one kind to another for quirky, personal reasons. We modify them. We want them not only to do a job but to express us, the attitude we take toward our job. So, too, with prose. We hunger for ceremony, for attitude, for ornament. It is no accident that bureaucrats play games with buzz words, build what amounts to purely ornamental patterns. These games express an attitude, albeit an ironically despairing one, toward what they are doing, the spirit in which they work. Jargons are created, too, for the same reason, to express a mystique, the spirit in which work is conducted. And, like a student's incoherence, they have their own eloquence, are clear about a habit of thought, a way of doing business. When we object to the prose, we are really objecting to the habit of thought, the bureaucratic way of life. It is because, paradoxically enough, the style is so clear, so successfully communicates a style of life, that we so object to it.

We have two choices, then, in regard to prose. We can allow the expression of personality and social relationships and try to control them, or we can ban them and try to extinguish them. Perhaps we should try the first alternative for a while. We've tried the second for the better part of a century and we know where it leads. It leads to where we are now, to the Official Style. For the do-it-yourselfer who wants to improve his prose, the choice is even clearer. Even if society disregards the importance of words, you must go in the other direction, train yourself to notice them and to notice them first. A style that at first seems peculiar may not be a "bad" style but simply eloquent about an unexpected kind of reality, one that you may or may not like. Try to keep clear in your mind when you are responding to the words and when to the situation they represent. You'll find that you do first the one and then the other. You'll be rehearsing the same kind of oscillation we have already found to be at the base of stylistic revision. You'll have trained your pattern of attention in just the same way that an artist trains his eyes or a musician his ears. After all, you can't revise what you can't see. Only by learning to see the styles around you can you go beyond a fixed set of rules, a paramedic procedure. In fact, in the long run, that is what any fixed set of rules ideally ought to do. It ought to start you out in training your verbal vision, to show

69

you how to *expand it*. Rules, analytic devices, are a shortcut to vision but no real substitute for it. The paramedic analogy here breaks down. Beyond paramedicine lies medicine; beyond the specific analysis of specific style—what we have been doing here—lies the study of style in general. Verbal style can no more be fully explained by a set of rules, stylistic or moral, than can any other kind of human behavior. Intuition, *trained* intuition, figures as strongly in the one as in the other. You must learn how to see.

Prose style, then, does not finally come down to a set of simple rules about clarity, brevity, and sincerity. It is as complicated as the rest of human behavior and this because it is part of that behavior as well as an expression of it. People who tell you prose style is simple are kidding you. They make reading and writing grotesquely simplistic. They make it unreal. Students often complain about the "unreality" of their school life, but just where it is most real—in the central act of verbal expression—they most yearn for simplification. Well, you can't have it both ways. You can choose the moralizing, rule-centered world, with the simplistic static conception of self and society, but you must not be surprised, when you try to use it in the real world, if it seems "unreal" in theory and backfires in practice. The other road is harder. You have to read and write and pay attention to both. If you do, you'll begin to see with what finesse we can communicate the subtleties of behavior. You'll begin, for the first time, to become self-conscious about the language you speak and hence about the society you live in. You will become more alive. And you'll begin to suspect the real answer to the question, "Why bother?" Because it's fun.

CHAPTER 6

Prose Composition and the Personal Computer

When, in the summer of 1978, tired and vexed from what seemed a lifetime of reading student prose, I sat down to write the original *Revising Prose,* I didn't know what a word processor was. I wrote on a yellow pad, as fast as I could, until writer's cramp overtook me—usually about four hours later—and I had to quit for the day. When I had the manuscript drafted, I spent three weeks revising it, blotting out whole sections with a magic marker, rewriting others, cutting and pasting, often block-printing phrases that my execrable handwriting had rendered unreadable. The manuscript was then typed and I read the typescript against the manuscript to make sure it had been typed correctly. I then revised the typescript just as I had done the manuscript, and it was retyped. And for large sections, again revised and retyped.

At that time, the "personal computer," as it came to be called, was little more than a toy in some kid's garage. Like the dedicated word processor, it was a device of whose very existence I was unaware. Yet the two devices, when put together, were to revolutionize the subject of this book, revising prose. I am writing these words at home, on an electronic screen, at five-thirty on a Sunday morning and will by evening, *deo volente,* complete a revision cycle that used to take six weeks. And the revising is not only quicker but easier and much more fun.

The electronic word is going to revolutionize not only prose revision but prose itself, how we write it, read it, and theorize about it. Even in a short, practical, hands-on manual like this one, we'll have to think for a moment about this revolution, simply because it has so transformed the subject that anyone who writes must know what has happened. And a lot more has happened than a mere change of means, from ink to electron.

In the nineteenth century, when typesetting was cheap, authors could revise from galley proofs. When typesetting became so expensive, writers made do with the typewriter. Now we can use a word processor, by far the most agile and easy revising tool ever invented. But whatever the technology, the aim has been the same—distance. To see your words in type automatically distances them, allows you to see them through someone else's eyes. And, of course, the personal computer on which the word-processing program runs can go further than this, transform the diagnostic procedures of the Paramedic Method into a regular on-line continuing check-out procedure for your prose. Michael Cohen and I have tried to show how this might be done in "HOMER," a revision program designed to accompany *Revising Prose.* Other prose revision programs are available and more are sure to appear. All will make prose revision easier and more fun than ever before. Any word-processing program allows you to put a single sentence before you on the screen and look *at* it rather than *through* it to the meaning beneath, to see what shape and size it has assumed, what it may sound like, how it relates actor and action. You can do the same thing on paper, of course, but on a computer screen the sentence somehow presents itself more self-consciously, invites revision rather than simply endures it.

The Paramedic Method, then, lends itself easily to computerization. The marriage promises well; consummate it as soon as you can. But several of the PM's targets—rhythm, tone, voice—cannot be addressed directly through a printed book such as this. They need color, graphics, animation, and sound, all interactively presented to a freely-responding reader. I tried to show, in the two television cassettes made to accompany the *Revising Prose* books ("Revising Prose" and "Revising Business Prose"), what a boon to prose analysis color digital videographics could be. They make revision a live process, one in which eye and ear cooperate fully with the mind. These animated print techniques, now available on advanced personal computers, will shortly come to the garden variety home machine. Together, these possibilities are redefining what writing prose means, how and why it is done, and especially how it is revised. Since the first edition of this book originally appeared, the world of prose and prose revision has metamorphosed; uncharted ground lies before us, unknown but extremely exciting.

Allegorical Alphabets

This book is not the place to illustrate these possibilities. In the first place no *book* can; the book is just what they are transcending. In the second place, *Revising Prose* is a hands-on guide, not a theoretical discussion. But perhaps just one example can suggest the changes in store for us: consider the revolution in *typography* which the personal computer is bringing about.

The printed book, as we have known it since Gutenberg, depends on print as essentially transparent and unselfconscious. We do not *notice it as print*. The book may be well designed or ill, and we may register that. But the kind of type selected, the size and shape of the letters, the white space between and around them, does not form part of the meaning. Making all these selections, "specing type" as the editors call it, is an editing, a production, task, not an authorial affair.

All this is now changing. Typography can now be—and I think increasingly will become—*allegorical,* part of the meaning, an authorial not an editing function. This will allow us to *see* prose characteristics that formerly we could only *talk about.* We will be able to analyze and revise prose in new ways, using new mixtures of alphabet and icon. We can begin to see how this process might work by using the type font and graphics capabilities of the commonly-available Apple Macintosh computer.

Here is the kind of academic sentence students read all the time:

> The integration of a set of common value patterns with the internalized need-disposition structure of the constituent personalities is the core phenomenon of the dynamics of social systems.

Huh? The usual shapeless shopping bag of general concepts held together by "is" and prepositional glue. Here are three diagrams of its structure, diagrams anyone can construct on the Macintosh.

The integration
of a set
of common value patterns
with the internalized need-disposition structure
of the constituent personalities
is the core phenomenon
of the dynamics
of social systems.

The	**integration**	of a set
of	**common value patterns**	
with the	**internalized need-disposition structure**	
of the	**constituent personalities**	
is the	**core phenomenon**	
of the	**dynamics**	
of	**social systems.**	

74

The		**Integration** of a set
of	**common value**	**patterns**
with the	**inter.need-disp.**	**structure**
of the	**constituent**	**personalities**
is the	**core**	**phenomenon**
of the		**dynamics**
of	**social**	**systems.**

In the first, I have done one of our usual vertical preposition charts, but with a little enhancement to render the pattern more graphic. The second chart tries to see what relationship the general terms bear to one another by listing them separately from the prepositions that glue them together in a string. The separate listing shows you immediately what is wrong; the concepts in the list bear no discernible relationship to one another. Nothing in the concepts themselves tells us how they might be related; the pressures for connection fall entirely on the prepositions. They cannot bear it. Their breakdown makes the passage so hard to read. And the qualification of the key terms by adjectives, which themselves represent key terms—"common value patterns," "internalized need-disposition structure," "constituent personalities"—makes things still worse. So I rearranged the sentence into the third chart, trying to isolate the key words all by themselves and indicating, by type-size, the importance of the three basic levels that compose the sentence. The lack of any fundamental relationship, causal or otherwise, between the central words in the right-hand column shows up even more. You can, given the syntax of the sentence, rearrange the central terms several different ways and still make sense of a sort. Try it.

Charts like this provide a powerful analytical tool. You needn't sit there cudgelling your brains in paralytic silence. You can start trying to make sense of things right on the screen. The need to "spec type" stimulates you to see how the sentence really fits together. And you can, by type selection, both display your analysis and demonstrate your attitude toward it. I've tried, for example, to make the first chart slightly satirical, the second and third graphically analytical only. Does it work? (I cannot, even after the analysis, make out what the sentence is trying to say and so cannot suggest a revision.)

Here is a simpler sentence altogether: "These ideas create a frame for the paragraph." A series of typographical manipulations shows the stages of perception that follow from applying Rules 3 and 4 of the PM—finding the action and putting it in a single, simple verb.

These ideas 𝕔𝕣𝕖𝕒𝕥𝕖 𝕒 𝕗𝕣𝕒𝕞𝕖 𝕗𝕠𝕣 the paragraph.

These ideas create a 𝕗𝕣𝕒𝕞𝕖 for the paragraph.

These ideas 𝕗𝕣𝕒𝕞𝕖 the paragraph.

These ideas frame the paragraph.

I used a "drop-shadow" typeface, one that frames each letter, to echo the "framing" action of the sentence. This kind of punning comment is just one of many available when type selection can be an authorial rather than an editorial function.

In the next example, I changed type to show just where, in mid-sentence, the reader gets lost. The second type selection tries to depict this confusion visually.

ORDINARY TYPOGRAPHY

However, consciousness does exist and it stimulates an antagonistic relationship between the acceptance of the role of self-consciousness and the disregard of the knowledge which is indigenous to consciousness for the adaptation of a more sentimental role.

ALLEGORICAL TYPOGRAPHY

However, consciousness does exist and it stimulates an antagonistic relationship between the acceptance of the role of self-consciousness and the disregard of the knowledge which is indigenous to consciousness for the adaptation of a more sentimental role.

It is easy to visualize the "shun-word" pattern:

We seek the key through recognition and rejection of arbitrary limitations placed on our potential.

And you can use a similar technique to spotlight a persistent sound-clash pattern, here a hissing "s," "sh," and "t" pattern in the prose of a biologist whose prose remains persistently tone-deaf.

Since Darwin initially provided the means of testing for the existence of an evolutionary process and for its significance in accounting for the attributes of living organisms, biologists have accepted with increasing decisiveness the hypothesis that all attributes of life are outcomes of that simple process.

In the next example, also written by a professor, I've tried to portray graphically the shapeless, unfocused prose by printing the passage three times, in typefaces that become progressively easier to read. The first makes us look at the shape of the sentence only, since it is so hard to read the typeface. The second is easier, the third easier still. It yields, in turn, to our usual graph of the shopping bag sentence. I've tried to satirize the wallboard monotony by making the prepositions huge and, with a glance at the medieval subject of the passage, in a "medieval" type.

It is one of the paradoxes of the history of rhetoric that what was in Antiquity essentially an oral discipline for the pleading of law cases should have become in the Middle Ages in one of its major aspects, a written discipline for the drawing up of quasi-legal documents.

It is one of the paradoxes of the history of rhetoric that what was in Antiquity essentially an oral discipline for the pleading of law cases should have become in the Middle Ages, in one of its major aspects, a written discipline for the drawing up of quasi-legal documents.

It is one of the paradoxes of the history of rhetoric that what was in Antiquity essentially an oral discipline for the pleading of law cases should have become in the Middle Ages, in one of its major aspects, a written discipline for the drawing up of quasi-legal documents.

It **is** one

of the paradoxes

of the history

of rhetoric that what **was**

in antiquity essentially an oral discipline

for the pleading

of law cases should have become

in the Middle Ages

78

in one

of its major aspects, a written discipline

for the drawing up

of quasi-legal documents.

I've asked students repeatedly how they read large stretches of "Official Style" academic prose; the uniform answer has been "I skip from key term to key term and try to guess at their connection." I've tried to depict this habit in the next sentence:

The idea of **action language implies** as the correct approach to the emotions **foregoing** the use of **substantives in** making **emotion-statements** and **employing** for this purpose only **verbs and adverbs** or adverbial locutions.

This kind of built-in "highlighting" provides a handy guide for revision. It may, too, find its way into the printing conventions for wallboard prose like this. Probably it would prove too satirical but it might, maybe, lead to revision before printing.

In the following typographical rendering, I've tried to depict visually a sentence slowly running out of gas as it passes through its prepositional phrase string. I've used italics at the end to emphasize how the central concept in the sentence has been placed in the least emphatic place possible, just before the sentence peters out completely.

Heartfelt has earned a

reputation for excellence for the sharing of the wisdom of the path *of compassionate service* in the natural healing arts.

Diagramming prose rhythm in a printed book never works very well; it goes against the grain of the medium. I was trying, in the following chart, to visualize a sentence whose first half was metronymically monotonous but whose second half fell into a very rhythmical, indeed even symmetrical pattern. I also thought it might show how a change in typeface can sometimes indicate a quotation more forcefully than quotation marks.

While the whole world even Roosevelt
felt a sense of relief
at the escape from war
at the time of Munich

Churchill stood up in the House of Commons and
disregarding a storm of protest
somberly declared

We have sustained a total and unmitigated defeat.

This last example springs from pure play. I had picked out this sentence from a student paper—"Etching will always be my love"—because it sounded silly to me. Should it be "I will always love etching"? Not much better. I wondered what typographical enhancement might do to it:

Etching will always be my love.

Etching will always be my love.

Etching will always be my **love**.

𝕰tching will always be my love.

No luck. It just seems to get sillier and sillier. Can you figure out why?

I've presented these typographical transformations as tools of analysis, but they are tools of creation as well, of course, and no doubt will be used as such when computer composition becomes commonplace. (How about the sound pattern in the last four words of the sentence I have just written?) The electronic word will mix creation and criticism, writing and revision, finally reading and writing themselves, which will alternate constantly in an interactive medium. Interactive computer fiction—detective games and the like—are doing this already. The whole idea of a fixed text, the center of the Western literary canon (at least since the Renaissance), now stands under attack. And our conception of the book—fixed, noninteractive, linear, black-and-white—seems due for transformation as well. I have no idea where this cornucopia of changes will fetch us up, but clearly prose—and prose revision—will never be the same. Revising the electronic word will be easier, more challenging, creative, and much more fun. The kind of typographical manipulation and commentary we've been toying with provides just a hint of the coming metamorphosis of the word.

With it will come a new understanding of prose style and, indeed, a new definition of prose itself. Let me close this brief prophetical excursus by suggesting how these changes will come about. We don't really digress in considering them, for they stand central to what *revising* prose will mean as well.

Traditional prose, as an artistic medium, operates by rigorous self-denial. It works by giving away most of its artistic repertoire and then earning it back the hard way. It permits itself no color, no allegorical typographical manipulations of the kind we've just considered, no visual arrangements that allow the eye to help the mind. Only linear, unvarying, black-and-white print. Within this self-denying convention, it then builds back the effects it has denied easy expression. It employs what used to be called the "colors of rhetoric," figures of speech that suggest balance, antithesis, parallelism, climax, patterns of sound, sometimes even colors. These figures of speech tension the prose, put the linear convention

81

under pressure, try to force from it the direct expression it has abjured. This tension drives prose, provides (let me practice what I preach) its principal propellant. I'll use a sentence by Samuel Johnson to illustrate the point. Here is how it looks in conventional print:

> But it must be strongly impressed upon our minds, that virtue is not to be pursued as one of the means to fame, but fame to be accepted as the only recompence which mortals can bestow on virtue; to be accepted with complacence, but not sought with eagerness.

Look what happens when we let some of those pressures for pattern find direct expression:

But it must be strongly impressed on our minds

that Virtue is not to be pursued

as one of the means to Fame

but Fame to be accepted

as the only recompence
which mortals can bestow on Virtue

to be accepted with complacence

but not sought with eagerness.

We feel as if we have broken the sentence open. We can literally *see* what it is about, how it works. Typography connects like words with like. But at the same time the prose has *lost power.* The power flows from the renunciation that our depiction dissolves.

The powers bestowed upon the electronic word thus enable kinds of creation that take us to the center of prose style. The kinds of depiction we have been doing suggest what a genuine theory of prose style must be built on—an understanding of its central act of renunciation. At the same time, that renunciation will change. Thus, we find a genuine theory of prose—we have, until now, lacked one—just at the moment when prose itself changes into something else.

This sketch of theory belongs in a practical, hands-on revision manual like this one because the techniques of revision, when dealing with the electronic word, introduce theoretical issues immediately and essentially. If we understand these theoretical issues, revising prose will be easier, faster, and more comprehensible. Prose revision of the electronic word, all this is to say, has become not only more fun but more profound—almost, one is tempted to say, a new thing altogether. It promises to be an exciting time for writers.

Terms

You can see things you don't know the names for, but in prose style as in everything else it is easier to see what you know how to describe. The psychological ease that comes from calling things by their proper name has been much neglected in such writing instruction as still takes place. As a result, students usually find themselves reduced to talking about "smoothness," "flow," and other meaningless generalities when they are confronted by a text. And so here are some basic terms.

Parts of Speech

In traditional English grammar, there are eight parts of speech: verbs, nouns, pronouns, adjectives, adverbs, prepositions, conjunctions, interjections. *Grammar,* in its most general sense, refers to all the rules that govern how meaningful statements can be made in any language. *Syntax* refers to sentence structure, to word order. *Diction* means simply word choice. *Usage* means linguistic custom.

Verbs

1. Verbs have two voices, active and passive.

An *active verb* indicates the subject acting:
  Jack *kicks* Bill.

A *passive verb* indicates the subject acted upon:
  Bill *is kicked* by Jim.

2. Verbs come in three moods: indicative, subjunctive, and imperative.

   A verb in the *indicative mood* says that something is a fact. If it asks a question, it is a question about a fact:

   > Jim *kicks* Bill. *Has* Jim *kicked* Bill yet?

   A verb in the *subjunctive mood* says that something is a wish or thought rather than a fact:

   > If Jim *were* clever, he *would* kick Bill.

   A verb in the *imperative mood* issues a command:

   > Jim, *kick* Bill!

3. A verb can be either *transitive* or *intransitive*.

   A *transitive verb* takes a direct object:

   > Jim kicks *Bill*.

   An *intransitive verb* does not take a direct object. It represents action without a specific goal:

   > Jim *kicks* with great gusto.

   The verb "to be" ("is," "was," etc.) is often called a *linking verb* because it links subject and predicate without transmitting a specific action:

   > Jim *is* a skunk.

4. English verbs have six tenses: present, past, present perfect, past perfect, future, and future perfect.

   > Present: Jim *kicks* Bill. (Present progressive: Jim *is kicking* Bill.)
   > Past: Jim *kicked* Bill.
   > Present perfect: Jim *has kicked* Bill.
   > Past perfect: Jim *had kicked* Bill.
   > Future: Jim *will kick* Bill.
   > Future perfect: Jim *will have kicked* Bill.

   The present perfect, past perfect, and future perfect are called *compound tenses*.

5. Verbs in English have three so-called *infinitive forms: infinitive, participle,* and *gerund.* These verb forms often function as adjectives or nouns.

Infinitive: To kick Jim makes great sport. ("To kick" is here the subject of "makes.")

Participles and gerunds have the same form; when the form is used as an adjective, it is called a *participle;* when used as a noun, a *gerund.*

Participles. Present participle: Jim is in a truly *kicking* mood. Past participle: Bill was a very well-*kicked* fellow.

Gerund: Kicking Bill is an activity hugely enjoyed by Jim.

(When a word separates the "to" in an infinitive from its complementary form, as in "to directly stimulate" instead of "to stimulate," the infinitive is said to be a *split infinitive.* Most people think this ought not to be done unless absolutely necessary.)

Verbs that take "it" or "there" as subjects are said to be in an *impersonal construction,* e.g., "It has been decided to fire him" or "There has been a personnel readjustment."

Nouns

A noun names something or somebody. A proper noun names a particular being—Jim.

1. Number. The singular number refers to one ("a cat"); plural to more than one ("five cats").

2. Collective nouns. Groups may be thought of as a single unit, as in "the army."

Pronouns

A pronoun is a word used instead of a noun. There are different kinds:

1. Personal pronouns—e.g., I, me, you, he, him, them.

2. Intensive pronouns—e.g., myself, yourself, himself.

87

3. Relative pronouns—e.g., who, which, that. These must have *antecedents,* words they refer back to. "Jim has a talent (antecedent) that (relative pronoun) Bill does not possess."
4. Indefinite pronouns—e.g., somebody, anybody, anything.
5. Interrogative pronouns—e.g., who?, what?

Possessives

Singular: A worker's hat. Plural: The workers' hats. ("It's," however, equals "it is." The possessive is "its.")

Adjectives

An *adjective* modifies a noun, e.g., "Jim was a *good* hiker."

Adverbs

An *adverb* modifies a verb, e.g., "Jim kicked *swiftly.*"

Prepositions

A *preposition* connects a noun or pronoun with a verb, an adjective, or another pronoun, e.g., "I ran *into* her arms" or "The girl *with* the blue scarf."

Conjunctions

Conjunctions join sentences or parts of them. There are two kinds, coordinating and subordinating.
1. Coordinating conjunctions—e.g., and, but, or, for—connect statements of equal status, e.g., "Bill ran and Jim fell" or "I got up but soon fell down."
2. Subordinating conjunctions—e.g., that, who, when—connect a main clause with a subordinate one, e.g., "I thought *that* he had gone."

Interjection

A sudden outcry, e.g., "Wow!"

Sentences

Every sentence must have both a subject and verb, stated or implied, e.g., "Jim (subject) kicks (verb)."

Three Kinds

1. A *declarative sentence* states a fact, e.g., "Jim kicks Bill."
2. An *interrogative sentence* asks a question, e.g., "Did Jim kick Bill?"
3. An *exclamatory sentence* registers an exclamation, e.g., "Like, I mean, you know, like wow!"

Three Basic Structures

1. A *simple sentence* makes one self-standing assertion, i.e., has one main clause, e.g., "Jim kicks Bill."
2. A *compound sentence* makes two or more self-standing assertions, i.e., has two main clauses, e.g., "Jim kicks Bill and Bill feels it" or "Jim kicks Bill and Bill feels it and Bill kicks back."
3. A *complex sentence* makes one self-standing assertion and one or more dependent assertions, subordinate clauses, dependent on the main clause, e.g., "Jim, who has been kicking Bill these twenty-five years, kicks him still and, what's more, still enjoys it."

In *compound sentences,* the clauses are connected by *coordinate conjunctions,* in *complex sentences* by *subordinate clauses.*

Restrictive and Nonrestrictive Relative Clauses

A restrictive clause modifies directly, and so restricts the meaning of the antecedent it refers back to, e.g., "This is the tire *that blew out on the freeway.*" One specific tire is intended. In such clauses the relative clause is *not* set off by a comma.

A nonrestrictive clause, though still a dependent clause, does not directly modify its antecedent and is set off by

89

commas. "These tires, which are quite expensive, last a very long time."

Appositives

An *appositive* is an amplifying word or phrase placed next to the term it refers to and set off by commas, e.g., "Henry VIII, *a glutton for punishment,* had six wives."

Basic Sentence Patterns

What words do you use to describe the basic syntactic patterns in a sentence? In addition to the basic types, declarative, interrogative, and exclamatory, and the basic forms of simple, compound, and complex, other terms sometimes come in handy.

Parataxis and Hypotaxis

Parataxis: Phrases or clauses arranged independently, in a coordinate construction, and often without connectives, e.g., "I came, I saw, I conquered."

Hypotaxis: Phrases or clauses arranged in a dependent, subordinate relationship, e.g., "I came, and after I came and looked around a bit, I decided, well, why not, and so conquered."

The adjectival forms are *paratactic* and *hypotactic,* e.g., "Hemingway favors a paratactic syntax while Faulkner prefers a hypotactic one."

Asyndeton and Polysyndeton

Asyndeton: Connectives are omitted between words, phrases, or clauses, e.g., "I've been stressed, destressed, beat down, beat up, held down, held up, conditioned, reconditioned."

Polysyndeton: Connectives are always supplied between words, phrases, or clauses, as when Milton talks about Satan pursuing his way, "And swims, or sinks, or wades, or creeps, or flies."

The adjectives are *asyndetic* and *polysyndetic*.

Periodic Sentence

A periodic sentence is a long sentence with a number of elements, usually balanced or antithetical, standing in a clear syntactical relationship to each other. Usually it suspends the conclusion of the sense until the end of the sentence, and so is sometimes said to use a *suspended syntax*. A perfect example is the passage from Lord Brougham's defense of Queen Caroline quoted in Chapter 3. A periodic sentence shows us a pattern of thought that has been fully worked out, whose power relationships of subordination have been carefully determined, and whose timing has been climactically ordered. In a periodic sentence, the mind has finished working on the thought, left it fully formed.

There is no equally satisfactory antithetical term for the opposite kind of sentence, a sentence whose elements are loosely related to one another, follow in no particularly antithetical climactic order, and do not suspend its grammatical completion until the close. Such a style is often called a *running style* or a *loose style,* but the terms remain pretty vague. The loose style, we can say, often reflects a mind *in the process of thinking* rather than, as in the periodic sentence, having already completely ordered its thinking. A sentence so loose as to verge on incoherence is often called a *run-on sentence*.

Isocolon

The Greek word means, literally, syntactic units of equal length, and it is used in English to describe the repetition of phrases of equal length and corresponding structure. Preachers, for example, often depend on isocolon to build up a rhythmic pattern or develop a series of contrasting ideas.

Falstaff parodies this habit in Shakespeare's *I Henry IV*: "Well, God give *thee the spirit of persuasion* and *him the ears of profiting,* that *what thou speakest may move* and *what he hears may be believed,* that *the true prince* may, for recreation sake, prove *a false thief."* And later in the play, "Harry, now I do *not* speak to thee *in drink but in tears, not in pleasure but in passion, not in words only, but in woes also."*

Chiasmus

Chiasmus is the basic pattern of antithetical inversion, the *AB:BA* pattern. The best example is probably from President John Kennedy's first inaugural address:

$$A \qquad\qquad B$$
"Ask not *what your country can do for you,* but

$$B \qquad\qquad A$$
what *you can do*   *for your country.*

Anaphora

When you begin a series of phrases, clauses, or sentences with the same word, you are using anaphora. So Churchill during the fall of France in 1940: *"We* have become the sole champion now in arms to defend the world cause. *We shall* do our best to be worthy of this high honor. *We shall* defend our island home, and with the British Empire *we shall* fight on unconquerable until the curse of Hitler is lifted from the brows of mankind. *We* are sure that in the end all will come right."

Noun Style and Verb Style

Every sentence must have a noun and a verb, but one can be emphasized, sometimes almost to the exclusion of the other. The Official Style—strings of prepositional phrases and "is"—exemplifies a noun style *par excellence.* Here are three examples, the first of a noun style, the second of a verb style, and the third of a balanced noun-verb mixture.

1. There is in turn a two-fold structure of this "binding-in." In the first place, by virtue of internalization of the standard, conformity with it tends to be of personal, expressive and/or instrumental significance to ego. In the second place, the structuring of the reactions of alter to ego's action as sanctions is a function of his conformity with the standard. Therefore conformity as a direct mode of the fulfillment of his own need-dispositions tends to coincide with the conformity as a condition of eliciting the favorable and avoiding the unfavorable reactions of others. (Talcott Parsons, *The Social System* [Glencoe, Ill.: Free Press, 1951], p. 38)

2. Patrols, sweeps, missions, search and destroy. It continued every day as if part of sunlight itself. I went to the colonel's briefings everyday. He explained how effectively we were keeping the enemy off balance, not allowing them to move in, set up mortar sites, and gather for attack. He didn't seem to hate them. They were to him like pests or insects that had to be kept away. It seemed that one important purpose of patrols was just for them to take place, to happen, to exist; there had to be patrols. It gave the men something to do. Find the enemy, make contact, kill, be killed, and return. Trap, block, hold. In the first five days, I lost six corpsmen—two killed, four wounded.   (John A. Parrish, *12, 20 & 5: A Doctor's Year in Vietnam* [Baltimore: Penguin Books, 1973], p. 235)

3. We know both too much and too little about Louis XIV ever to succeed in capturing the whole man. In externals, in the mere business of eating, drinking, and dressing, in the outward routine of what he loved to call the *metier du roi,* no historical character, not even Johnson or Pepys, is

93

better known to us; we can even, with the aid of his own writings, penetrate a little of the majestic façade which is *Le Grand Roi*. But when we have done so, we see as in a glass darkly. Hence the extraordinary number and variety of judgments which have been passed upon him; to one school, he is incomparably the ablest ruler in modern European history; to another, a mediocre blunderer, pompous, led by the nose by a succession of generals and civil servants; whilst to a third, he is no great king, but still the finest actor of royalty the world has ever seen.   (W. H. Lewis, *The Splendid Century: Life in the France of Louis XIV* [New York: Anchor Books, 1953], p. 1)

Patterns of Rhythm and Sound

Meter

The terms used for scanning (marking the meter of) poetry sometimes prove useful for prose as well.

> *iamb:* unstressed syllable followed by a stressed one, e.g., iñ·vólve.
> *trochee:* opposite of iamb, e.g., áṁ·bēr.
> *anapest:* two unstressed syllables and one stressed syllable, e.g., thēre hē góes.
> *dactyl:* opposite of anapest, one stressed syllable followed by two unstressed ones, e.g., óp·ēr·āte.

These patterns form *feet.* If a line contains two, it is a *dimeter;* three, a *trimeter;* four, a *tetrameter;* five, a *pentameter;* six, a *hexameter.* The adjectival forms are *iambic, trochaic, anapestic,* and *dactylic.*

Sound Resemblances

Alliteration: This originally meant the repetition of initial consonant sounds but came to mean repetition of consonant sounds wherever they occurred, and now is often used to indicate vowel sound repetition as well. You can use it as a general term for this kind of sound play: "Peter Piper picked a peck of pickled peppers"; "Bill will always swill his fill."

Homoioteleuton: This jawbreaker refers, in Latin, to words with similar endings, usually case-endings. An English analogy would be "looked" and "booked." You can use it for cases like this, to describe, for example, the "shun" words— "function," "organization," "facilitation"—and the sound clashes they cause.

For further explanation of the basic terms of grammar, see George O. Curme's *English Grammar* in the Barnes & Noble College Outline Series. For a fuller discussion of rhetorical terms like *chiasmus* and *asyndeton,* see Richard A. Lanham's *A Handlist of Rhetorical Terms* in the University of California Press's Campus Paperback Series.